PENGUIN BOOKS

WHY VOTE LIBERAL DEMOCRAT?

William Wallace (Lord Wallace of Saltaire) is Reader in International Relations at the London School of Economics and Professor of International Studies at the Central European University in Budapest. He completed his five-year term as Walter F. Hallstein Senior Research Fellow at St Antony's College, Oxford, in the summer of 1995. From 1978 to 1990 he was Director of Studies at the Royal Institute of International Affairs in London, responsible for the Institute's research and publications programmes.

He speaks for the Liberal Democrats in the House of Lords on foreign affairs and defence questions.

Why Vote Liberal Democrat?

William Wallace

PENGUIN BOOKS

PENGUIN BOOKS

Published by the Penguin Group
Penguin Books Ltd, 27 Wrights Lane, London W8 5TZ, England
Penguin Books USA Inc., 375 Hudson Street, New York, New York 10014, USA
Penguin Books Australia Ltd, Ringwood, Victoria, Australia
Penguin Books Canada Ltd, 10 Alcorn Avenue, Toronto, Ontario, Canada M4V 3B2
Penguin Books (NZ) Ltd, 182–190 Wairau Road, Auckland 10, New Zealand

Penguin Books Ltd, Registered Offices: Harmondsworth, Middlesex, England

First published 1997
10 9 8 7 6 5 4 3 2 1

Set in 10.5/12.5pt Monotype Sabon
Typeset by Rowland Phototypesetting Ltd,
Bury St Edmunds, Suffolk
Printed in England by Clays Ltd, St Ives plc

Contents

Foreword

Why vote at all? Long before you choose among the candidates on the ballot paper, you (like many others) may well be tempted to stay at home this time. Spin doctors and political journalists dominate the national campaign, adopting the techniques of American presidential campaigning to persuade half-listening voters that their leader is trustworthy while their opponents are dangerous. Sound-bites on television and advertising slogans seek to suggest that there are simple choices to be made between the parties, and few hard choices to be made between incompatible objectives: that you can have *both* tax cuts *and* decent public services, *both* freedom to do what you want yourself *and* the chance to stop others from doing things you don't approve of.

No government in the last fifty years has represented the majority of the British electorate. Labour returned to office in 1974 on 37 per cent of the vote. The Conservatives gained office in 1979 on 44 per cent, and held on to office in the three subsequent elections with 42 per cent or less. In almost three out of every four constituencies the result is a foregone conclusion, with a candidate already chosen by a small group of party members guaranteed a seat in the next Parliament. Computer-aided campaign techniques enable party campaigners to concentrate on the limited number of 'swing voters' in the crucial 150 seats which will decide the outcome. The Conservatives sent out 'personal' letters in September 1996 from John Major to this key group: 2½ million people out of an electorate of 43 million. You are most likely not one of these 'swing voters', on whom the election is seen to depend; so why not give it all a miss?

I want to persuade you that it is worth your while this time to vote – and to vote Liberal Democrat. Your vote, and those of millions of others, can move British politics away from the dreadfully sterile confrontations of House of Commons debates and away from the limited agenda on which the Conservatives and 'New' Labour have chosen to fight. The larger the Liberal Democrat vote, the stronger the Liberal Democrat presence in the House of Commons, the more the closed world of Westminster politics will be forced open.

Yes, Britain has a remarkably undemocratic political system, which has been taken under more and more central government control over the past twenty years – but with your help, we can clean it up and open it up. Yes, Britain's economy suffers from remarkably low rates of private and public investment, with government selling off public assets to finance current spending and with new employment heavily dependent on investment by foreign companies; with your help, we can promote a longer-term approach. Yes, education and training has been held back in Britain compared to our competitors abroad; with your help, we will give it greater priority.

Yes, Britain is a more divided country than it was a generation ago, with a widening divide between rich and poor, between young and old, between those in the inner cities and those outside; with your help, we will rebuild an inclusive national community. Yes, British government has so far neglected the environmental dimension, pressing ahead with free market policies without considering long-term sustainability and environmental costs; with your help, we will bring the environmental dimension into the centre of taxation policy, planning, energy use, economic regulation and foreign policy. Yes, British politics and British newspapers have sunk into nostalgic nationalism; with your help, we will instead promote Britain's long-term interests through European and global cooperation.

ONE

Our Political Approach

Political choices are fundamentally about values: what sort of society you prefer to live in, what trade-offs you make between your private interests and the interests of society as a whole, what balance you would strike between individual freedom and social order or between individual wealth, public goods and redistribution to others within the community. Democratic politics in Britain often looks a rather sleazy business, where ambitious young men (they *are* almost all men) go into Parliament to make money out of ministerial connections and honest people do better to stay outside. There *is* a great deal wrong with British national politics at present. The structure of Britain's political institutions is one of the underlying issues in the coming election campaign, on which Liberal Democrats argue for radical changes – as I explain in Chapter Three. Aside from the mechanisms of politics, though, different political groups stand for distinctive approaches to political values. Margaret Thatcher's political assumptions and values differed very clearly from those of the Labour Government she followed, and differed also from those of the 'one nation' Conservatives around her predecessor, Edward Heath. Over a period of eleven years in office, the strength of those beliefs gradually altered the shape of Britain's society, government and economy. A different government would have taken Britain in a different direction, for better or for worse. So we have to start with underlying beliefs and principles.

Good government requires a careful balance to be struck

between three linked elements: state power, market economy and society. State power provides the framework of law and order which markets need to work efficiently and which societies need for security. Markets allow economic innovation and promote economic efficiency, with the added political and social value of allowing a wide degree of choice to a large proportion of individuals. Societies provide continuity, community and culture, the glue which holds people together. These three of course closely interact. Societies promote and pass on the values which inform both market and state; where social ties weaken, order is threatened and the state must step in. Market economies provide the resources on which states rely. Too much state interference will distort markets and build in inefficiency; non-intervention in accordance with 'free-market' principles will allow the strongest players to distort the markets. When the state becomes too strong, civil society and individual liberty are threatened; when the state is too weak, private wealth buys corrupt influence.

The preamble to the Liberal Democrats' party constitution sums up our approach. We

exist to build and safeguard a fair, free and open society, in which we seek to balance the fundamental values of liberty, equality and community, and in which no one shall be enslaved by poverty, ignorance or forced conformity . . . We recognize that the independence of individuals is safeguarded by their personal ownership of property, but that the market alone does not distribute wealth or income fairly . . . These are the conditions of liberty and social justice which it is the responsibility of each citizen and the duty of the state to protect and enlarge.

Not *one* fundamental value, but three: not *just* liberty without regard for resulting inequality, nor enforced equality at the expense of individual liberty, nor authoritarian community without room for individual diversity. Each qualifies and limits the other. Absolute liberty is anarchy, destructive of the order we need for social life; absolute equality destroys individual expression and initiative. We seek to keep these different objectives in balance by working to build an open society, supported by a wide dispersal of property and income in a market economy, protected and policed by a government with carefully limited powers, politically accountable to its citizens. That crucial balance is our political philosophy.

Different times, different needs

Where that balance of values and objectives should be struck, and how it should be adjusted as economic and social circumstances change, is one of the central questions of democratic politics. Economic and technological changes alter the relationship between market, society and state; so do social changes, such as the growth of cities and the decline of the village or the shifting balance between young and old.

The early Liberals were concerned above all to limit the power of the authoritarian state. The 'new Liberals' and social democrats of late-nineteenth-century Britain were more concerned to use government to correct the abuses of market capitalism and to tackle the poverty and disease of the industrial towns and cities. Twentieth-century Liberals promoted the mixed economy against socialists pushing for state control and free marketeers demanding that capitalism should be uncontrolled, and set out the principles of a welfare society to prevent the emergence of an excluded underclass. From the outset Liberals were internationalists rather than nationalists, seeing Britain's interests as best served through cooperation with other states rather than through rivalry and war. Now for the twenty-first century we place greater emphasis than ever on the necessity of international cooperation, in a world which is changing very rapidly and in which British governments cannot achieve economic or social objectives except through working with others.

The Liberal tradition in Britain grew out of the struggles between King, Parliament and people in the century after the English civil war. John Locke, the seventeenth-century Liberal philosopher, insisted (against supporters of the Stuart kings) that government existed by the consent of the governed, and that the power of the state should not be allowed to override the autonomy of civil society – defined as a society of free men based upon widely dispersed property and equality under the law.

Gladstone's Liberal Party built on this tradition. Liberals in government recognized that Britain's rapidly growing industrial economy could not be left to market forces alone, and introduced laws to regulate the use of children in factories, to limit working hours and to improve safety. Liberals in local government in the expanding cities and towns paved and lit streets, opened schools, built reservoirs to provide clean water, introduced gas (and later electricity) and trams as public services to the community.

The great philosopher of nineteenth-century Liberalism, John Stuart Mill, championed the cause of individual liberty – for women as well as for men – against the intolerance of closed societies and the oppression of authoritarian states. But he also argued that there is a positive role for government to play in expanding individual opportunity through education, in preventing destitution and in regulating markets. Government intervention, he added, should be as local as possible in its actions and in its links to those it serves; it should be clearly accountable, subject to rules, with authority dispersed among different institutions and offices. The principle he propounded was of 'the greatest dissemination of power consistent with efficiency'. Active government should be directed towards enabling all citizens to realize their potential skills and talents. 'The worth of a State, in the long run, is the worth of the individuals composing it . . .'

Gladstone's Liberal coalition split over three issues which still affect British politics: Ireland, free markets and empire. Against those who saw the sovereignty of Westminster, 'the Imperial Parliament', as unique and indivisible, the Liberal government proposed home rule for Ireland, and thereafter for Scotland and Wales, to bring power back to the national communities which make up the British state and to satisfy Irish grievances against rule from London. Whig landowners, fearing that home rule would affect their property rights, defected as 'Unionists' to the Conservatives, blocking political reforms which would have saved both Britain and Ireland a century of conflict.

In foreign policy Gladstone's Liberals and their successors were committed to international cooperation and free trade, against the imperialism of Disraeli's Conservatives. The reaction of Joseph Chamberlain and other manufacturers to the rise of German industrial competition was to call for a shift to 'imperial protection' against the European continent. Liberal Imperialists in their turn defected to the Conservative Party, supporting the scramble for colonies in Africa and the Boer War, and contributing to the nationalist and anti-European stream within the Conservative tradition which has come down through the League of Empire Loyalists of the postwar years to the Eurosceptics of today.

The great Liberal government of 1906 was thus based upon a different coalition from that of Gladstone fifty years before. Liberal free traders and municipal improvers had welcomed representatives of the working classes into their ranks as voting rights were extended, together with social reformers determined to build a stronger national community by extending a stake in that community to all its citizens. Lloyd George replaced the old Poor Law Boards with a scheme of 'national insurance' against unemployment and ill health, together with provision for a basic old-age pension. Local and national government strengthened regulations covering town planning, transport, sanitation and working conditions. The introduction of the probation service enormously reduced the prison population; national and local government worked together in improving education and health. This government of liberals, radicals, social democrats and labour representatives was probably the greatest reforming government which Britain has seen. It was, however, blocked by bitter Conservative opposition to renewed Liberal efforts to give Ireland home rule, and then destroyed by the outbreak of war in 1914 and the traumas which followed.

Between the wars and for a generation after 1945, Liberal and social democrat ideas flowed through governments of other parties, influencing the climate of British politics without sharing in its direction. John Maynard Keynes set out the principles of the mixed economy, and worked with Lloyd George on his 1928 'Yellow Book', *We Can Conquer Unemployment*. William Beveridge's lifelong work on poverty and social deprivation culminated in his 1944 Report, which was carried into practice by the 1945 Labour government in the establishment of the National Health Service and the creation of a 'welfare state'. Twice between the wars, in 1923 and 1929, the emerging Labour Party refused to agree a coalition with the Liberals; long periods of Conservative supremacy were therefore interrupted by short intervals of weak Labour government.

For a period after the Second World War it seemed almost as if political Liberalism had lost its historic role. A social democratic consensus between the Conservative and Labour parties, supported by steady economic growth, full employment and rising public expenditure, left the distribution of income, welfare and taxation, and the balance between public control and private enterprise, as the main divide between the two parties. The breakdown of that consensus from the late 1960s on, and the failure of both these parties to adjust to changing economic and social circumstances, has provided the foundation for the re-emergence and growth of the Liberal Democrats as an increasingly influential third force in British politics.

Plural politics, open politics

It was always an illusion that the diversity of issues in British politics could be squeezed into a simple division between two parties. Right and left, government and opposition, blue and red, conjure up false images of a mass society divided down the middle: between capital and labour, employers and unions, middle class and working class, rich and poor. Britain came closest to this two-way division between classes in the 1950s, the era of mass trade union membership, mass employment in heavy industry, and deference to authority. The dominating issues in politics were economic. The Labour Party stood for state control and redistribution, and the Conservatives stood for private enterprise and lower taxes – though each adopted a sufficiently moderate approach to share a good deal of common ground in between.

The nostalgia which many older people today feel for the 1950s reflects their recollection of an age when choices seemed simpler and loyalties were straightforward. But the transformation of Britain's economy and society since then has made political choices much more complex, and attempts to compress them into a simple 'either–or' ever more artificial. Both the Conservative and Labour Parties today are coalitions of different attitudes and approaches. 'One-nation' Conservatives like Kenneth Clarke coexist uneasily with free-market evangelists like Michael Portillo and John Redwood. 'New Labour' enthusiasts like Harriet Harman sit as uneasily with old Labour loyalists like John Prescott and Clare Short. But even to suggest that each of these parties can be divided into two opposing wings is too simple. Even on the Conservative right some are libertarian, wanting to take the state out of social control and regulation; others are authoritarian, calling for stricter government policies to enforce morality, restrict divorce and crack down on crime. Some within the Labour Party, like Jack Straw, are close to these elements on the right on social issues, though not on economic; others, like Chris Mullen and Ken Livingstone, are left-wing libertarians. Both Labour and Conservative Parties contain internationalist *and* nationalist tendencies, both pro-European *and* anti-European. The result is to make some of the central questions for British politics taboo for both these suppressed-coalition parties, as too internally divisive to risk public debate.

The Liberal Democrats also bring together a range of views, of different priorities and perspectives, around common principles and values. We don't expect you, in your turn, to agree with every item in our current manifesto; you as an individual voter will have your own priorities and beliefs. We hope to persuade you, however, that our overall approach is the most appropriate for Britain as it enters the twenty-first century, and offers you the best opportunity to give your hopes, ambitions and preferences a political voice. One of the distinctive character-istics of the Liberal Democrats, which attracted many of us into this political party and holds us together, is a particular open and tolerant political style. We believe that the way politicians approach government – cooperative or antagonistic, open or exclusive, informative or populist – is in many ways as important as the promises they offer.

What is most distinctive about the Liberal Democratic approach, under Ashdown as under Gladstone, is our approach to political power. Conservatives see power as vested in the state, to be shared only with the market. Socialists used to think power should be exercised through the state on behalf of the people, over the market as well as over society, without much need for limits on what a government which claimed to represent 'the people' could do. Liberals see power as safely controlled only when widely dispersed and bound by clear rules. All power corrupts. Governments in power for too long, MPs peddling influence in the governing party, local authorities dominated by one party for a generation, companies which dominate their sector of the market, unions which control the supply of labour, directors whose shareholders fail to hold them accountable, newspaper magnates whose influence extends over television: all tend to abuse their position. Liberals therefore seek to spread power as widely as possible, to share between different levels of government, to involve as many citizens and groups within society as possible; and the exercise of power must be accountable to those over whom it is exercised.

The supposed necessity of giving Britain 'strong government' has been the basis of two-party politics in Britain over the past fifty years. Any government with a parliamentary majority has been able to push through what it wants, subject only to the sanction of losing office at the next election, from the abolition of the Greater London Council to the Dangerous Dogs Act and the Poll Tax. The result has been a mass of ill-considered legislation and an increasing centralization of control over local communities. This didn't start with Mrs Thatcher's government. A previous Labour government pushed through a similarly untested and half-thought through tax (Selective Employment Tax, or SET), with similarly disastrous results. A future Labour government with a clear parliamentary majority might well be tempted to behave in the same 'strong' fashion. That's why Liberal Democrats place such a high priority on constitutional reform, to negotiate a new political settlement to give Britain accountable and fully democratic government. We prefer good government to 'strong' government.

Now that state socialism has been discredited, the main alternative to liberal democracy is the libertarian approach: to cut down the state and leave matters to the market. Michael Portillo's Barcelona speech two years ago summed it up well:

It has been argued that the free market is a jungle to be tamed by governments. It is at least as plausible that governments are a jungle to be tamed by the free market.

Ideological libertarians like Portillo discard concepts like social justice and social order, in pursuit of which governments tax and regulate market behaviour; for them, the rationality of the market and the freedom it gives to individuals to make what they can is enough. We argue against this near-anarchical free-market doctrine that market power, as much as state power, must be subject to regulation and control to prevent the establishment and exploitation of dominant positions. Market power, furthermore, can be translated into political influence. Rupert Murdoch through his newspapers is pursuing his own political agenda, while Sir James Goldsmith (like Ross Perot in the USA) has even attempted to buy himself a political party.

Past Labour governments took far too large a proportion of the national economy into the public sector, creating an over-mighty state which cramped private enterprise. Conservative government since 1979 has taken the state out of some aspects of the economy, but has given central government more authoritarian and arbitrary power over society. The idea of a public service, of a politically neutral administration serving not only the government of the day but also the longer-term interests of the country, has been compromised; ministers have even attacked the independence of the judiciary and courts. Britain, like any other democratic country, needs state institutions which command the respect of society as a whole, including the respect of its government. Our proposals for political reform are intended amongst other purposes to restore that relationship of mutual respect. The balance within a mixed economy between public provision and private enterprise is not, for Liberals, a matter of unyielding ideology but of choices to be made on utilitarian grounds – choices which may need to change in response to economic, technological and social changes. The free-market insistence that privatization is always and in all circumstances better than public provision seems to us as absurd and irrational as the old Socialist belief that state control was under all circumstances better than private enterprise.

Civil liberty matters as well as political liberty. Intolerant societies oppress minorities and eccentrics as much as market domination and state control. Individual freedom of expression safeguards diversity, widens choices and blocks the imposition of yesterday's conventional wisdom as today's unyielding orthodoxy. All societies have a tendency towards intolerance, towards excluding social deviants by labelling them as immoral or disruptive, even mad. Those who defend the importance of strong civil societies, with a wide diversity of organizations and groups independent of the state, need to be wary of the dangers of social exclusion, of communities which define their interests without regard to those of others, of groups which reinforce their identity by stressing their superiority to the 'others' from whom they distinguish themselves. For Liberals, every citizen matters: minorities as well as majorities, women as well as men, black British as well as white, the unemployed as well as those in work. We resist the pressures of the moral majority to force others to conform to their social values. Strong communities need not be intolerant communities; diversity of opinion and expression builds an open society, capable of change and development.

The fullest possible development of each individual citizen's potential has been a firm Liberal principle since the eighteenth-century Enlightenment. Education, as Mill argued, is the key to individual fulfilment; its provision is a duty shared between individual, society and state. State provision of education helps to bind together society and nation, bringing up future citizens with a sense of the wider community they belong to. Education is also the key to economic prosperity; the quality of labour input, its technical skills, its openness to innovation, is as vital as the input of capital and – in the contemporary global economy – more vital than raw materials.

Liberty without property, without some resources for living, is destitution. Citizens without income or employment for long periods lose their stake in society and in the state which claims their loyalty. State, society and market all benefit from the widest possible distribution of wealth, opportunity and employment. State welfare which does nothing more than subsidize an unemployed underclass drains public expenditure without bringing this economically excluded group back into active participation in society. A stable and open society cannot be built or maintained without providing all citizens with the prospect of employment. As competition and technological change sweep away old jobs, government must work to encourage the market to offer new employment, by shifts in the burden of taxes and through changes in market regulation, and should help those out of work to acquire the skills they need to return to work. The quickening pace of technological change and the global nature of economic competition has made it more necessary to be able to move from job to job, and more difficult in many cases to acquire the new skills needed. The top priority which Liberal Democrats give to public provision of education and training responds to this need.

This election, like the last, risks descending into a competitive auction between promises of low taxation. Liberal Democrats have an instinctive preference for low taxation, like limited government; the state should be allowed to collect and spend no more than is clearly needed for the public good. Gladstone made his reputation as a reforming Chancellor of the Exchequer, determined to cut out waste and to limit unnecessary spending. 'Peace, retrenchment and reform' were the three linked principles of mid-nineteenth-century Liberalism. Retrenchment – cutting back on public expenditure – went naturally with peace, against Conservative governments determined to expand military spending in pursuit of national grandeur, and with reform against Conservatives using public money to benefit their friends through patronage.

Taxation is, however, the contribution every citizen makes towards living in a civilized society. It is not, as some right-wing Conservatives argue, to be cut without regard to the social consequences; nor, as old Labour used to assume, is it to be raised to pay for whatever schemes those currently in power wish to promote. Britain, like other advanced industrial societies, now has a growing elderly population and a smaller proportion of people in work paying taxes to support their health care and pensions. Britain needs a more highly educated workforce to compete in a changing world market. Over the past twenty to thirty years we have been living off the public assets which our parents and grandparents paid for without reinvesting in return. No arbitrary figure of tax cuts to be imposed addresses these questions. Promises of tax cuts offer voters immediate satisfaction and long-term disillusion, as they discover that cuts in public provision force them to pay more out of their own pocket – if they can afford it. The Liberal Democrat principles are: no taxation without explanation, no taxation without justification. Government must be more open with its citizens as taxpayers, in linking taxes raised to public goods provided.

Paddy Ashdown's Liberal Democrat coalition contains a strong green element. Nineteenth-century Liberals were concerned to improve the urban environment. This generation of Liberal Democrats has learned the importance of bringing concern for the environment – urban and rural, local, national and global –

into every aspect of government. Liberal Democrats in local government throughout Britain have taken the initiative in raising environmental standards, in promoting energy saving and recycling. But there is much which can be achieved only through national action and international cooperation, through shifting assumptions about economic growth and exploitation of resources, and through shifting the basis of taxation to reflect environmental costs – rather than to increase labour costs, as at present. Our state, our economy and our society are handed on to us in trust from our parents, to be handed on in turn to our children. Government should not operate within a five-year span, living and planning from one election to another. Good government must make policy for the long term, and must invest for the long term.

Liberals from the outset have been internationalist, as I have already noted. They promoted free trade and open frontiers because they believed contact and cooperation led to peace, while protection and nationalism led to war. The commitment to internationalism, to overcoming national hostility through trade and cooperation, led Liberals after the Second World War to welcome proposals for European integration. Commitment to closer European cooperation and through that to international cooperation, against the idea of socialism in one country, was a primary motive for those Social Democrats who left the Labour Party to combine with the Liberals fifteen years ago. Liberals and Social Democrats campaigned throughout the 1950s and 1960s for the rights of the colonial peoples whom Britain was still governing, and after that to support the economic and political development of newly independent countries and to work for a multiracial, democratic and open society in southern Africa against the apartheid regime.

For us, internationalism now means working through partnership in Europe to promote global cooperation. The rapid integration of the global economy over the past twenty-five years, the equally rapid deterioration of the global environment, the additional strains on international order imposed by the rise in world population, the proliferation of small and weak states and the break-up of the Soviet empire, make international cooperation even more vital – and nationalist reassertion even more damaging to our long-term interests.

Political influence, political power

This is all very well, you may say, but does it really matter what Liberal Democrats think? Britain has a two-party system, and, whether you like it or not, the choice to be made is between Labour and the Conservatives. Well, not necessarily: the two-party system has already weakened a great deal. In one constituency in three in this election the battle for first place is *not* between Labour and Conservative. In many the Liberal Democrats are the main challengers to the Conservatives; in some we are the main alternative to Labour. If you want to see real change in British politics – not just a change of government but a change of system – you will need to deny *both* Labour and Conservatives the absolute majority they demand.

That's not as difficult as you may think. Already in the 1992 general election forty-four of the 651 MPs elected to Westminster came from outside the two established parties: twenty Liberal Democrats, seven Scottish and Welsh Nationalists, seventeen from the different parties of Northern Ireland. This may seem a poor return for the quarter of the votes cast which they won, but Britain's single-member constituency system best rewards those whose votes are concentrated in particular seats. Now there are fifty MPs from outside the two main parties, twenty-six of them Liberal Democrats, our numbers boosted by by-election successes and disillusioned moderate Conservatives who have crossed the floor to join us. Seventy-five to a hundred such MPs next time, backed by the legitimacy of a large nationwide vote, will mean an end to the domination of closed coalitions operating as single-party government – a fundamental change therefore in the style and behaviour of government and the issues it has to address.

But, you may add, there's no reason to believe that Liberal Democrats would behave differently from anyone else if we gained political influence or a share in power. Why should you believe that we want to take power in order to disperse it, when you have seen so many governments take power and then gather more privileges around them? I can offer you three answers to reassure you. First, the Liberal Democrats are a group of people who came into politics preferring principles to office, who did not choose the easier Conservative or Labour route because we were – and are – determined to put our own policies into practice rather than to jump on the nearest bandwagon or dress in the latest political fashion. If we had gone into politics just to make a career, we would have joined a different party.

Second, you can judge by the Liberal Democrat record in local government throughout the country. Liberal Democrats now control fifty-five local authorities – more than the Conservatives – and share power in a further seventy-one; they are responsible in total for budgets which amount to £14 billion and for 650,000 employees. Where we have taken power we have shared it, have helped local communities to govern themselves. We have implemented Liberal Democrat priorities, economic, social and environmental, as far as is possible within the tight constraints of central controls over local government and central financing.

Third, the political reforms we are proposing will make it easier for you to catch us out if we are going off the rails, and to throw us out if we get too accustomed to power. Open government, with information more freely available, will enable you as a citizen to understand much better what your government is doing and to check on its record. Shared power, with a stronger Parliament to counterbalance the government in office and to hold ministers to account, will force any government over which we have influence to explain and to justify its actions. We too might grow corrupt if left in undisputed power for too long; which is why we are determined to alter the rules of government to ensure greater democracy and public accountability. The Liberal Democrats, as our deputy leader Alan Beith has remarked, are the only party asking for office so that they can reduce its powers. Britain is now the most secretive and centralized state among the industrialized democracies, with the least representative government. We will use our influence, from the moment we gain it, to redress that democratic deficit.

Politics in the round

Manifestos at elections carry lists of policy proposals, assembled into sections marked 'The Economy', 'Our Society', 'The Nation's Health', 'Foreign Affairs' and so on. It's easy for the casual voter to pick and choose those items which appeal, and ignore the rest, without stopping to consider how these different dimensions fit together. But politics and government need to be seen in the round. The pattern and level of taxation adopted impacts upon economic development, and often on social behaviour and choices as well. The foreign policy pursued feeds back into costs of defence and diplomacy, as well as into opportunities and obstacles for trade. Transport policy affects energy needs and has environmental consequences; land-use planning, the permitted development of towns and cities, housing estates, industrial plants and shopping centres, has evident implications for transport needs. Successful promotion of new employment requires extra expenditure on training, but will save much more on social security. Crime goes up when unemployment goes up; the costs of unemployment thus also spread across the police and the legal system into the overflowing prisons. Cuts in spending now may win an election, but lead to higher spending on delayed investment and maintenance later – perhaps for your children to pay.

Part of the deterioration of political debate in recent years has been the shift from detailed explanation to short slogan, from radio discussion to television sound-bite. For professional politicians trying to capture the attention of a sceptical and half-interested electorate, such short cuts are essential and unavoidable. A century or more ago large crowds of working men were willing to stand in the open for a couple of hours to listen to Gladstone holding forth on the principles of public expenditure or the maltreatment of the Bulgarians by the Turks. Their much more affluent grandchildren and great-grandchildren sit comfortably at home, their fingers hovering over the television remote control to switch channels if the prime minister goes on for too long. You who have picked up this book and persevered this far through it will, however, understand that politics can only be reduced to lists, slogans and sound-bites at the cost of immense over-simplification; and that the underlying issues and the links between them require more careful and considered thought.

So the chapters which follow cut across the conventional divisions between issues, looking forward well beyond the next election and Parliament and glancing further back than the last five years. Before that, however, we need to examine the context within which any British government, of whatever political colour, will have to operate – the rapid and radical changes which set the limits to political choice.

TWO

Small World, Rapid Change

Politics is not just about winning elections, arguing over choices for the next four or five years. It should also address long-term issues, asking how well we have used the assets we inherited and how much we are reinvesting for the benefit of our children and grandchildren – and for ourselves for the rest of our lives. If you are now in your forties, you may well have another fifty years to look forward to living in this country, relying on the quality of its society and its public services and on the ability of its economy to pay for them. If you are now under twenty-five, voting in your first or second general election, your own life expectancy should give you an interest in the state of Britain and of the world as far forward as 2060–70.

The world has changed more rapidly over the past fifty years than in any previous era. It will change as rapidly over the next fifty. If we are successful in building institutions for international cooperation, in altering unsustainable patterns of consumption and use of natural resources, in checking the rise in world population, we will have achieved a peaceful world and a sustainable global economy. If we fail, then we face the likelihood of severe environmental degradation and an increasing struggle over scarce resources in a hostile world.

You may say that there is little that we in Britain can do about all this, and that your vote should be decided by immediate personal interests and concerns. But the policies which the British government follows will strengthen – or weaken – international cooperation, and may even alter the direction of international cooperation. What happens outside Britain directly affects our economy and its prospects, our security and our way of life. Those of us who are fifty or younger have been lucky to grow up in an era in which Western Europe was at peace, in which disorder and conflict elsewhere in the world affected us very little, and in which most people in Britain grew better off year by year. The British standard of living doubled between 1945 and 1970, and will have doubled again by the year 2000. But neither the British nor the world economy can go on growing at the same pace and in the same way for another twenty-five or fifty years. Economies in Asia are now developing rapidly, competing for raw materials and markets and adding to the global pollution for which the developed countries of Europe and North America have so far largely been responsible. Global climate change resulting from rising air pollution will affect the British Isles as directly as the rest of the world; we *have* to find ways to reshape the global economy. Technological change destroys and creates jobs in Britain as in other countries; you need intelligent government to help Britain's economy and society to adjust.

Within Britain as well, long-term changes underlie current political issues. The shift over the past generation away from an economy based on manufacturing to one based on services, from shipbuilding and steel-making to consumer goods and electronics, has increased the importance of skills and retraining and altered national patterns of employment and unemployment. The rise in life expectancy and the decline in the birthrate are leading to a very different balance between young and old, with implications for the balance of taxation and public expenditure. The rising demand for health, social security and pensions, and the increasing reluctance of those in work to pay the taxes needed to provide them, has led some to talk about inter-generational conflict replacing class conflict as the future dividing line in democratic politics. Changes in family structure and in the status of women have altered patterns of social dependence and interdependence, and increased demands upon the local community or the state to provide welfare.

Political debate which ignores these underlying changes misleads the public. We should not pretend that we can somehow regain past patterns of employment or family life, or that taxes can be cut without considering rising demand for services. We have to start from where we are, and where we expect to be in five, ten, fifteen years' time and beyond.

The second industrial revolution

The British economy thirty years ago was still primarily a manufacturing economy, still dominated by British-owned companies and British state-owned industries. Coal remained the country's most important source of primary energy, coal-mining one of its largest sources of employment. Steam engines were still pulling trains on British Rail, though steam was giving way to diesel. Cunard ships carried more passengers across the Atlantic than BOAC planes; international direct dialling from Britain to other countries was slowly becoming available, but its high cost meant that most businesses, as well as private individuals, continued to rely on written mail.

Foreign companies manufacturing in Britain relied on domestic suppliers for most of their components – international sourcing was for most components too slow, too unreliable and too expensive in transport costs. Ford of Britain thus produced entirely different models from Ford of Germany, Vauxhall from Opel – designed in Britain, not controlled from Detroit. Electric typewriters and calculators were gaining acceptance in banks and offices, alongside their manual counterparts; there was only a small number of computers in use in Britain, and they were huge, expensive and – by today's standards – painfully slow. Few British citizens travelled beyond their national borders for work, study or pleasure. International mass tourism took off only with the advent of cheap charter flights at the end of the

1960s; seaside holidays in Britain were then challenged for the first time by seaside holidays in Spain.

By contrast the British economy today has become an intrinsic part of an integrated European market, which itself interacts intensively with North America and East Asia within a fast-moving global economy. Much British-owned industry collapsed in the first three years of Mrs Thatcher's government, when the Conservatives allowed the sterling exchange rate to rise by a third. Manufacturing in Britain has been rebuilt since then largely through inward investment, by Japanese, German, Korean, Swedish, American and Taiwanese companies. British-based multinationals have redefined themselves as European companies operating in the global market; British Ford and Vauxhall are now part of integrated European manufacturing and marketing operations, assembling vehicles to common designs from components shipped in and out across the continent.

The electronic revolution has supported the rise of new, largely foreign-owned, concentrations of industry in Scotland, the north-east and Wales – their new assembly plants attracted by British and European Union subsidies to the desolate sites left by the collapse of coalmines and steelworks. The impact of electronics on the service sector, most of all upon financial services, has been as radical. Local branches of banks and building societies have long since lost their autonomy, and now depend on central management and central computers. Plastic cards, almost unknown thirty years ago, enable customers to check their accounts and withdraw money from them throughout Britain – and for many also while abroad. The City of London competes for global trade with Tokyo and New York, managing financial transfers at a speed and on a scale beyond the comprehension of their 1960 predecessors. International mass tourism – and the heritage industry – has become one of Britain's most profitable service providers and one of its largest employers, while British citizens explore new holiday destinations in North America and west Africa, the eastern Mediterranean and the Indian Ocean.

This pace of change seems more likely to quicken than to slow down over the next ten to twenty years. The costs of international transport and communications are continuing to fall. The power of computers is rising even more rapidly than their cost is falling, making desktops and laptops tools of the job for much of the working population. Satellite television and the Internet are spreading fast, but still penetrate only a small proportion of their potential market. New industrial materials – advanced ceramics, carbon fibre – are beginning to alter established industries and to open up the potential for new products. Genetic engineering offers huge opportunities, and also huge risks. Financial markets are experimenting with new derivatives, and painfully discovering the risks they bring with them. Scientific research and technological innovation offer the prospect of other changes, from electric cars and cheap solar energy to nuclear fusion.

The transformation of the British and world economies has also made for a transformation of work. Few can now look forward to holding the same job throughout their working life, as many of their grandfathers did; most will need to continue to learn new skills in order to remain employable. Automation of industrial production is shrinking the number of jobs available in industry, leaving more and more people dependent on the expanding service sector for employment. One British worker in four is now a part-timer, two out of five are outside permanent employment – providing flexible labour in the service sector and in small companies, their wages far behind the élite of technicians and managers whose skills are in most demand. One and a half million people now 'telework' from home on a regular or occasional basis, bringing new life into villages which have lost their traditional sources of employment – but impairing the social dimension of shared work.

For those who lack skills – most of all unskilled men, the core working class of the old industrial economy – it is becoming harder and harder to find work. Economic changes thus contribute to a widening gap between the successful and the unsuccessful. Increasingly affluent families in which both parents have well-paid jobs contrast with households in which no family member is in paid employment, leading to the re-emergence in Britain of a deprived underclass similar to that of the late nineteenth century.

The demographic revolution

A third of the world's population in 1900 lived in Europe or had emigrated from Europe over the previous fifty to 150 years. Europe had experienced a massive population explosion during the nineteenth century, as new agricultural methods were introduced, economic development created new towns and factories, and government acted to improve public health and child care. In the last fifty years Europe's population has stabilized, but the same processes of economic and political modernization have led to a comparable explosion in Asia, Africa and South America. World population had risen from somewhere around a billion (1,000,000,000) in 1800 to some 2 billion on the eve of the First World War. By 1950 it was 2.5 billion; and by 1990 it was well above 5 billion, increasing at a rate of nearly 90 million a year and unlikely to stabilize on the most optimistic estimates until 2050 or later.

Europe itself now accounts for less than 10 per cent of the world's population. The flow of migration has now reversed, with migrants struggling to reach the rich world as desperately as the European poor struggled to reach America or Australia a century ago. Rapid development combined with fast population growth has disrupted societies and states, as it did in several European states in earlier years. The fastest rates of population increase are in the Muslim world of the Middle East and north Africa, Europe's immediate southern neighbours; Algeria, for example, to which southern Europe was exporting its own surplus population a century ago, is likely to double its population within the next twenty-five years, with intelligent unemployed young having to seek work elsewhere. The population of Africa south of the Sahara is also projected to double within a twenty-five-to-thirty-year period, from 250 to 500 million, with potentially disastrous implications for the continent's delicate ecology and weak systems of government. China, still the world's largest country in terms of population, is likely to be overtaken by India within the next twenty years; northern India has for some time been an area of emigration, as rural populations crowd the land and cities overflow.

Britain's population, in contrast, is stable, and would have fallen without the influx of new immigrants and the higher birthrates of their families. To a degree which would have astonished our grandparents this has become a multiracial society, our ethnic minorities now making a valuable contribution to our economy and society, and a vital contribution to public services like health and transport. Rising life expectancy and a falling birthrate have radically altered the ratio of those in work to dependent pensioners – from 7:1 in 1945 to 3:1 in 1995, and an anticipated 2.2:1 in 2030. The number of pensioners is expected to rise by 50 per cent in the first thirty years of the next century. The 'fit retired' are already a familiar part of British society: carrying out many of the voluntary tasks which women undertook a generation ago, active in politics and interest groups. More and more men in their fifties are joining them, as companies resort to early retirement to cut overheads, or find it easier to take on school-leavers than to retrain higher salary earners already set in their ways.

The global shift from Europe to Asia

Our grandparents were born into a world of which Europe seemed unquestionably the centre and Britain one of the world's greatest powers. The British empire itself included a quarter of the world's population, in India, Africa, Australasia, the Indian and Pacific oceans, the West Indies and Canada.

Our parents were born into an American-led world, in which it was still easy to assume that Western culture and Western values were superior to those of other regions of the world, and that the future for the poor states of Asia and Africa lay in imitating Western economic and political models, hoping to follow where we had led. Britain as the 'mother country' of the Commonwealth retained the prestige of a global power. Representatives of newly independent states came to London to admire our Parliament and the strength of our democratic institutions; British MPs travelled to their capitals to present them with books on parliamentary procedure and copies of the Commons' mace. What we had lost in independent world status we had managed to maintain through the 'special relationship' with the USA: an 'independent' deterrent, which the Americans provided, and a posture of national sovereignty in relations with Europe which rested on the acceptance of dependence on the United States.

In 1960 the Americans and West Europeans together accounted for over two thirds of world production (conventionally measured); transatlantic trade dwarfed the trickle across the Pacific. Thirty years later, in 1990, East Asia accounted for 22 per cent of world production, against 29 per cent each for North America and Western Europe; trans-Pacific trade had overtaken transatlantic, with Taiwan, Hong Kong, Singapore and mainland China all significant exporters. Since then the Chinese economy has continued to grow at 8–10 per cent per annum – though the Japanese rate of growth has slowed. India is also emerging as a substantial regional economy, with an expanding affluent and educated urban middle class alongside mass urban and rural poverty. As Japan becomes a mature economy, with a balance between young and old approaching comparison with Europe, so Japanese companies have been moving offshore to invest and produce in the rest of East Asia. Overseas Chinese from Singapore, Indonesia and Taiwan have invested heavily in China, while also moving into California and British Columbia.

America is no longer an Anglo-Saxon country, run by men for whom England had been their spiritual home. Population movement within the USA, reinforced by immigration, has shifted the balance over the past thirty years from the east to the west coast. California is now by far the largest state, its mixed European–Asian–Hispanic population part of America's reorientation from the Atlantic community of the cold war era to the Pacific community of the Asia–Pacific Economic Council (APEC) and the preoccupation with its southern neighbours signalled by the inclusion of Mexico within the North American Free Trade Area (NAFTA) and by plans to extend NAFTA further to the south.

British foreign policy, like French, is based upon the assumption that we must maintain our global standing and status. The rise of East Asia, above all of China, increasingly questions that assumption. Japan long since overtook Britain and France together as a provider of international aid; the yen (together with the Deutsche Mark) long since replaced the pound sterling and the franc as a reserve currency. If China's phenomenal growth rate is successfully maintained past the beginning of the twenty-first century, the size of its economy (though not of course the GNP per head) will approach that of the USA.

European governments will have to consult and negotiate with these fast-growing countries as a group – as they have already begun to do in the Europe–Asia Dialogue, which John Major attended with other European heads of government last year. The illusion that Britain might somehow rediscover a special relationship with Asia as an alternative to closer European commitment, which floats around Conservative think-tanks and the right-wing press, ignores the evidence and the trends. Germany exports twice as much as Britain to China, and invests more heavily there and across East Asia; France also has a larger trade with Asia than Britain. The memory of an imperial Britain, in diplomatic relations with every territory from Kabul to Peking, means nothing to most of today's Asian population. Twenty-first-century Britain will find its interests in the most economically dynamic region of the world most effectively represented as part of a European group, within which the British government is an active and constructive player.

The transformation of Europe

The political balance of the European continent has altered fundamentally in the seven years since the Berlin Wall came down. For forty years from 1949 to 1989 Britain played a key role in the Atlantic Alliance. Geographically and politically America's closest ally in Europe, our navy patrolled the north Atlantic to protect the sea lanes from the Soviet submarine threat, while the bulk of our army and air force was committed to the defence of divided Germany from the Red Army.

Now the Soviet Union has collapsed, and the remains of the Red Army are struggling to maintain rusting equipment; 200,000 of the 300,000 American troops which were based in Western Europe, some of them in Britain, have also gone home, leaving the West Europeans to shoulder more of the responsibility for our own defence. Reunited Germany is now at the centre of a wider Europe, its economy weighed down by the costs of incorporating the 17 million people of former East Germany, but also responding to the economic opportunities opening up across its eastern border. Ten former socialist states, Poland the most important, are on their way to full membership of the European Union (EU), with Poland and several others likely to join within the next five years. Well before then it is likely that Poland will have been admitted to NATO, and that NATO will have signed a parallel agreement with Russia. This would convert the Atlantic Alliance into something rather closer to a Europe-wide security framework than the defensive alliance it was during the cold war.

The European Union has already begun to change shape. Austria, Sweden and Finland, neutral European states which had stayed outside the EU on political grounds during the cold war, joined the EU in 1995. Economic and technical assistance has flowed to central and eastern Europe, and patterns of trade have started to shift. Polish two-way trade with the EU rose by 40 per cent in 1995; West European, American and East Asian companies are investing heavily in Hungary and the Czech Republic.

Looking forward ten years or more, it is probable that the EU will have expanded to include some twenty-five to thirty countries, and NATO to some twenty to twenty-five. That will involve significant internal changes within both organizations, perhaps with an inner directing group emerging within the EU to compensate for the diversity and incoherence of the broader membership, very probably with a much stronger European entity within NATO to compensate for the USA's more limited commitment. Britain has the option to stay outside such a core group if our government insists upon maintaining national sovereignty. But the maintenance of sovereignty will be paid for in relegation to Europe's political periphery.

Much will depend on developments within Russia, on how active a role the USA remains prepared to play in Europe, and on the stability or instability of the countries to Europe's immediate south around the Mediterranean. But it is clear that the context for British foreign policy has shifted radically. The Atlantic framework within which it operated from the 1950s to the 1980s is widening out into a more complex European and global framework, within which Britain is no longer a central player.

Small world, endangered environment

Thirty years ago only oceanographers and meteorologists devoted much time or concern to the study of trends in world climate. Starting with small groups of politically active scientists in the 1970s, growing with both the accumulation of scientific evidence and the expansion of environmental movements in the 1980s, pressing in on governments over the past five years, has come incontrovertible evidence of global warming. It has been accompanied by satellite data and locally collected statistics of environmental degradation on land, in the air, among the world's stock of plant and animal life, and in the oceans.

The challenge of global environmental degradation poses threats that the current international system of nation states is ill-equipped to handle. Effective action to reverse the processes of climate change, for example, requires almost all the world's states to cooperate in developing and applying radical policies to avert a threat which may not become acute for several decades. Politicians are having to learn about the 'precautionary principle': that it is wiser to act on the basis of scientific uncertainty than to risk the irreversible consequences that worst-case scenarios might bring. Politicians and publics who are used to focusing on issues at most one to five years ahead are struggling to anticipate potential developments twenty-five to fifty years from now.

Traditional approaches to foreign policy do not fit this challenge. A new concept of national security is needed, bringing in non-military threats to the prosperity and stability of state and society – as Warren Christopher, then US Secretary of State, powerfully argued in a speech in the spring of 1996. Previously domestic policy choices – on the balance of taxation, on energy use, on land-use planning, on agricultural and forestry methods, on the disposal of waste – now have to be considered in terms of their impact on neighbouring states and on the broader global community. This implies that states which saw themselves as sovereign must now seek to intervene directly and deeply in the internal affairs of their neighbours, and are forced to accept that their neighbours may wish to challenge their domestic jurisdiction in return.

The scale of the environmental challenge to conventional assumptions about national sovereignty, economic growth and free-market economics is immense. Britain's Conservative government has begun to adjust, though it has lagged behind other north European states both in policy adjustments made and in willingness to explain the issues at stake to our citizens. UN estimates indicate, for example, that a reduction of 60 per cent in emissions of carbon dioxide, the main greenhouse gas, will be necessary to stabilize its concentration in the atmosphere after decades of rising emissions. Yet most industrialized countries, including Britain, are committed only to limit CO_2 emissions to 1990 levels.

The most easily understandable and manageable aspect of environmental degradation has been the depletion of the ozone layer: originally detected over Antarctica, it is now also occurring over Europe in the spring and summer. The Montreal Protocol on the elimination of chlorofluorocarbons (CFCs) represents an encouraging example of states working together to impose agreed regulations. It has, however, sparked an extensive illegal international trade in CFCs, requiring police forces and customs officers to work together closely to combat an international crime which represented legitimate trade a mere five years ago.

The most vivid and immediate evidence of environmental degradation is in the developing world. Over-exploitation of limited water supplies for irrigation has shrunk the Aral Sea to 40 per cent of its size in 1960, while rising extraction from international rivers – the Nile, the Euphrates, the Tigris, the Jordan – threatens inter-state conflict in Africa and the Middle East. Deforestation and desertification have damaged parts of Latin America, Africa and Asia; almost 30 per cent of India's land is now classified as degraded beyond productive use. Tropical rainforests in Zaire and the Amazon basin are being rapidly destroyed, threatening to destroy with them their rich habitat of plants and animals. Population growth is exacerbating environmental degradation. International organizations and aid agencies are therefore under pressure to assume an increasingly active posture towards the countries responsible. But the UN and many of its agencies are at the same time under increasing attack from within the United States, while Britain as a permanent member of the UN Security Council wavers between loyalty to international cooperation and reluctance to criticize its American ally.

Environmental problems are not, however, confined to developing countries. Within Britain, intensive farming methods are inflicting serious damage on the soil, particularly in areas of intensive farming such as East Anglia. Water quality is of particular concern, after decades of under-investment in the water industry. In 1989 the EC began proceedings to prosecute the British government for failing to comply with water-quality directives. The accelerating growth of road transport is creating local air-quality problems similar to those of southern California. British energy efficiency is well below the standards of most other advanced industrial democracies. Countries downwind from Britain on the European continent have complained with increasing vigour about acid deposition from British emissions. Countries across the Channel and the North Sea have exchanged protests over coastal pollution and dumping at sea, and bargained with each other and with Britain over tighter controls.

Britain and the other industrialized nations have therefore to move towards building environmentally sustainable economies, built around a redefinition of economic priorities and of the components of economic growth, resource depletion and economic and social value. Efficiency in the use of energy and other primary resources will be one of the key determinants of successful economies in the future. Indeed some of the greatest opportunities for new wealth creation lie in investment in energy efficiency and renewables, in pollution-control equipment and recycling plant – all areas in which Britain currently lags behind our competitors. Major changes in our way of life – in our concepts of employment and work, in the way we use private cars, in where and in what way we build our homes, in how and where we shop, even in what we eat – will be needed.

For British voters over the age of sixty-five, such long-term considerations may be of interest only in so far as they may affect their children and grandchildren. For younger voters, however, the predicted effects of climate change in terms of rising sea levels and global warming may well plague their old (or even middle) age. Yet Britain's political institutions, built around a five-year electoral cycle and a stylized battle between two parties, with new issues and old compressed into the straitjackets of two-party politics, are poorly designed to allow for a shift of direction – either to adjust to changes already under way or to take precautionary action to avert predicted future problems. If you

Why Vote Liberal Democrat?

want to see British politics moving on to a new and more far-sighted agenda, then you will need to help the Liberal Democrats reshape the way British political institutions work.

THREE

Giving Britain Better Government

Are you happy about the way Britain is governed? Or do you see Parliament and national politics as sleazy and self-centred, in desperate need of reform? The answer you give positions you on one side or other of one of the central dividing lines in British politics. The Conservatives go into this election as defenders of Britain's unwritten constitution. Labour is in favour of restoring a parliament to Scotland and reviving local government, but wants to maintain the central structure of the state they hope to control. Liberal Democrats are committed to thorough reform.

Britain has inherited one of the world's oldest democratic traditions. Those who defend that tradition most strongly cling to the view that Britain remains more democratic than other countries, and that the superior quality of Britain's unwritten constitution sets us apart from the younger and less firmly established democracies on the European continent. The argument over constitutional reform within Britain is thus directly linked to national identity and to attitudes to Europe. It is linked also to the movement for self-government for Scotland and Wales. The British Parliament is the symbolic core of English nationalism, the Union which Conservatives and Unionists have defended for 120 years against efforts to allow first the Irish, then the Scots, to govern themselves within a less centralized United Kingdom.

Mrs Thatcher was fond of recalling that the British Parliament has a continuous 700 years' history – skating over its non-inclusion of the Scots for the first 400 years, and its non-democratic character for the first 550. Hugh Gaitskell when leader of the Labour Party rhapsodized about '1,000 years of British history', following the (now-forgotten) myth of the English Parliament as directly descended from King Alfred's Anglo-Saxon witan. Michael Portillo, English nationalist by adoption, has spoken of the beauty of a constitution which has slowly developed from century to century, and the dangers of destroying the whole by changing any of the parts.

Conservative rhetoric will make much of the 'threat' of constitutional reform in the forthcoming election. Their conviction that Britain's present political arrangements are in no need of change falls down, however, on four counts:

– first, their complacency about the current structure of British politics contrasts sharply with popular opinion. Opinion-poll evidence indicates widespread and rising public disillusionment. The percentage agreeing with a MORI poll statement that 'the present system of governing Britain mainly works well' dropped from 48 per cent in 1973 to 22 per cent in 1995, while those agreeing that it 'needs a great deal of improvement' rose from 49 per cent to 76 per cent.

– second, the Conservatives have themselves changed Britain's constitution quite radically over the past seventeen years: centralizing power away from local government, replacing elected representatives by appointed bodies, hiving off ministerial responsibilities into separate agencies and bending the rules of parliamentary accountability.

– third, there has been a succession of avoidable policy disasters and scandals – from secret and illegal arms sales to Iraq, to the failure to respond in time to the problem of BSE and press disclosure of businesses paying MPs to promote their interests and ask questions in Parliament on their behalf – which indicate that the current system is not working.

- fourth, there is a growing consensus from outside experts that political institutions designed for the simpler politics of a past age no longer meet the demands of contemporary government.

Redesigning the British state

The root of the problem is that a government with a majority in the House of Commons is able to do whatever it likes, from changing the relationship between central and local government to allowing the intelligence services to take on some of the responsibilities of the police. The doctrine of parliamentary sovereignty, which was developed in the seventeenth century in the course of the struggle between the Commons and the Stuart kings, concentrates *all* constitutional authority in Parliament itself. If Parliament wishes, one seventeenth-century lawyer argued, it could declare black white or pass a law making a man a woman. The House of Commons represented the nation, and the government – appointed by the king but answerable to Parliament – represented the state. No written constitution was needed because the Members of Parliament represented the practical common sense of England, combined with respect for English common law.

So long as the king's ministers were only a small group in the Commons, there remained a large degree of separation between Parliament and government. The American constitution, with its strict doctrine of the separation of powers between executive government, representative Congress, and judiciary, was modelled on contemporary British practice as they saw it, adding stronger controls on the executive and a written framework to substitute for the role played among the small political class in Britain by practice and precedent. But the growth of organized parties, of a mass electorate and of large-scale government has given parties in government effective control of the Commons and almost destroyed its original capacity for open debate. What we have now is what Mrs Thatcher's first Lord Chancellor, Lord

Hailsham, has accurately described as an 'elective dictatorship'.

The independent backbenchers who saw their role as holding the government to account for its actions have shrunk to a small minority. Nearly a third of the 651 members of the 1992–7 House of Commons are either members of the government or 'shadows' hoping to take their places soon; half the others are former ministers or front-benchers, or recent recruits doing what the Whips ask them in the hope of gaining promotion soon. The Labour front-bench team announced in August 1996 set a new record in locking MPs into government-seeking discipline: 101 shadow ministers and spokesmen, of whom eighteen are in the Whips' Office, as against ninety-seven Conservative ministers and Whips. Add to that another thirty 'parliamentary private secretaries' on each side, unpaid assistants whose apprenticeship to the ministers and shadow ministers whose bags they carry is the first step towards their goal of a ministerial post, and fully 40 per cent of the Commons is caught up in government or alternative government. The proper role of a democratic parliament is to provide a check on government, to question its proposals and actions, to hold it accountable to the public – not to serve as a waiting-room for ministerial office.

The twentieth-century justification for strong government based on two-party politics was that it gave the electorate a clear choice between one team and another, each with a programme set out in the manifestos on which they fought. In reality it was never that easy to compress all the issues at stake into two competing agendas. In recent elections what parties promised has borne less and less similarity to what they carry out when in power. The Conservative manifesto of 1979 gave no hint of the massive programme of privatization which they initiated in office. The Conservatives in 1992 promised lower taxation, only to raise taxes again after regaining power. Labour's draft manifesto for 1997 gives only the broadest hints of the direction which it would take once it gained office. The voter is asked in effect to choose between two teams, and to trust the one he or she chooses to pursue intelligent policies in office – without any effective checks on its behaviour until the next election. But all the evidence of opinion polls shows that fewer and fewer voters are prepared to trust politicians that far.

What is needed is a complete overhaul of the framework of British politics: a new constitutional settlement which will bring executive government under democratic control and open up the closed world of Westminster and Whitehall. Previous efforts to introduce piecemeal constitutional reforms – of the House of Lords in the 1960s, of self-government for Scotland in the 1970s – were lost in the pressures of competing government business and the resistance of traditionalist MPs to yielding up any of the Commons' privileges. Liberal Democrats therefore argue for a new approach, looking at the British constitution as a whole, taking away from the Commons the absolute right to legislate on any issue without any outside check.

We start with central government itself. The Conservatives promised to cut back on the state, but instead have taken power away from local authorities to the centre, pushed the civil service into playing an increasingly partisan role, and given ministers powers of appointment and direction over a vast growth of executive agencies, trusts and 'quasi-non-governmental bodies' (or QUANGOS). These spend an increasing amount of public money, but are beyond effective democratic control. Liberal Democrats want a smaller government, with fewer ministers; it is absurd that over the past four Parliaments the number of ministers has increased while the number of civil servants has shrunk.

A smaller government would itself contribute to a greater separation of Parliament from government. More fundamentally, however, we want to replace parliamentary sovereignty with a written constitution. This would spread power away from its current concentration in the leadership of whichever party controls the House of Commons; it would set down rules which even prime ministers would have to follow, with constitutional rules enforceable in the courts and open to amendment only by a two-thirds majority of both Houses of a reformed Parliament.

The different elements have to be considered together: a more independent House of Commons, recruited and elected through processes less directly under party control, return of the proliferation of agencies and boards which now spend such a large proportion of our taxes to democratic control through a revival of local government and the provision of elected parliaments for the nations of Britain and the regions of England, a Freedom of Information Act to give citizens the right to know what governments have done, with civil liberties entrenched in a Bill of Rights and enforceable through the courts. This is an ambitious programme. It is, however, what is needed to take Britain towards the democratic standards which every other advanced industrial state has attained over the past fifty years, while Britain has been moving in the opposite direction towards increasing secrecy and central control.

John Major proudly claimed in a speech in July 1994 that 'we are opening up the map of how Britain is governed. It's a big agenda, dwarfing any changes we've seen since the modern pattern of government was established.' This was, in effect, an anti-democratic revolution: transforming public services into market bodies, and citizens into consumers. The theory behind it was that the market provides each individual with greater freedom of choice, while removing politics from the provision of health, training, education and welfare. In practice it has seen the appointment of Conservative supporters to more than nine thousand paid jobs running these new bodies, which now spend £24 billion of taxpayers' money, and which operate without any clear line of constitutional or legal accountability. Any new government will have to tackle this network of patronage, restore democratic accountability and re-establish the boundary between public service and private profit.

Privatization was championed by the Conservatives as the primary means to shrink the state and to expand the role of the market. Under Labour public control had expanded far too far into industry; a shift in the balance was both healthy and desirable. Transfer to the private sector of functions previously exercised by the state has not, however, taken government completely out of their management. Government regulation of private gas, electricity and water companies provides a new forum for political choice and political influence. Where government provision of public subsidies to private companies is involved, as in the railway network, the boundaries between public interest and private profit are blurred. What was proposed as a strategy for reducing the role of government has in practice surrounded the government with lobbies and influence brokers, using their contacts with ministers to press forward the interests of their clients. As recent parliamentary scandals have revealed, we are sliding towards a patronage state in which money and connections buy private advantage, and in which companies that profit from government contracts employ Conservative MPs as consultants and contribute to Conservative party funds.

What we need are clearer rules, stronger parliamentary scrutiny, guaranteed access to information about government contracts (and party finances), contained within a written constitution. This would limit the government's ability to take decisions without reporting to Parliament and would provide the citizen with the right to challenge the government in the courts when rules are broken. But it is also important to reinstate the concept of public service as such, which the Conservatives have undermined, to return to the principles of a civil service which serves the state and the national interest as well as the government of the day. 'The primary duty of civil servants,' the Liberal Democrat Constitutional Declaration states, 'is to uphold the constitution'; they should not be forced to act as instruments of partisan government, or pushed into ambiguous relationships with private interests.

As with so many other aspects of politics, the reform of government needs to be seen in the round. Changing the way Parliament is recruited and elected will limit one-party control. Spreading authority between central, regional and local government will allow for smaller national government, and release Parliament from its present burden of detailed legislation to focus on wider and longer-term issues. Written constitutional rules, supported by freedom of information, will limit the executive's freedom to bend power to partisan or private advantage. Greater separation of Parliament from government will strengthen democratic accountability, and protect the civil service from ministerial pressures to cut corners and bend rules. Each will reinforce the other. Minor changes here and there, introduced by a single-party Labour government otherwise concerned to exercise the power it has won, will not be enough to clean up the mess and give Britain an open democracy.

Opening up our democracy

The style of British politics suited an age in which few voters considered themselves well enough informed to follow more than the broad outline of major political issues, in which mass party membership gave a substantial part of the electorate direct identification with their political leaders and in which a deferential national culture encouraged trust in distant leaders. Now that a third of eighteen-year-olds continue into further and higher education, now that television brings national and international news into our living-rooms, now that single-issue groups have overtaken all-purpose parties as mass-membership organizations, Britain needs a more open political structure.

Instead we are moving towards a presidential style of national politics, in which political leaders compete on image and television interviews while skating over the most central and sensitive issues which they will have to face in government. It is absurd to be approaching a general election in which the Conservative and Labour leaderships are conspiring not to explain to voters what is at stake in British membership of a single currency (a decision which any new government will have to face within months of taking office), nor to explore the implications for public services and pensions of cutting or raising taxes, nor to discuss openly the whole issue of climate change and environmental sustainability and its implications across the whole range of national policies.

Two-party politics, in Britain as in America, presses the diversity of political life into a competition between leaders and disciplined teams round a narrow and artificial agenda. In both countries television has worsened the distortion, as the personality of each leader and the discipline (or indiscipline) of their team has become a central part of the 'story' political journalists report. Left-wing socialists, one-nation conservatives, younger voters, environmentalists, those passionate about animal welfare, are squeezed out, represented if at all only as discontented minorities on the fringes of each party coalition.

Party control of nominations for parliamentary seats, most of them safe enough for nomination to guarantee election, restricts choices further. The narrow path towards political advancement starts with student politics, moving on through catching the eye of patrons within the party leadership to adoption as a candidate, a well-behaved period as a parliamentary backbencher and then the prospect of ministerial office. So South African Peter Hain is sent to occupy a seat in Wales, and Londoner Peter Mandelson to represent Hartlepool. So political campaigns target a small proportion of voters in a small number of seats, tailoring the issues that are raised to what are seen as their interests. And so an increasing proportion of the voters shift allegiance to campaigning groups outside Parliament, and many do not bother to vote at all.

A more open system of voting, which allows each voter a greater choice among different candidates, is thus an essential aspect in recapturing politics from party control. When local authorities have been reorganized, with three candidates from each party nominated for each ward, it has been striking how much more often a diversity of candidates has been presented, including a large proportion of women and of locally strong ethnic groups – because the parties understand that that is what many voters want. Where choice is limited in a single-member constituency, most party associations go for middle-class men. The strongest single reason why Britain has fewer women MPs than any other Parliament in Europe is that we have the least representative systems of nomination and election.

It is a sad reflection of the limited imagination of the Labour leadership that it has been willing to impose the selection of women on particular constituency parties in order to reduce the male domination of Parliament, but hesitates to approve a more open electoral system which would give voters some say in which candidate from which party they choose. A couple of hundred Labour or Conservative party members – all that there are in many of the constituencies they hold – is far too narrow a base to control recruitment into Parliament. That is why Liberal Democrats insist on a referendum on electoral reform, and will argue for a change to a system (as in Ireland) which elects several Members of Parliament from larger constituencies to represent more of the diversity of attitudes and origins in Britain's society.

Such a change would contribute to a more open Parliament, in which the power of party Whips to control business and suppress alternative views would be weakened. A multi-party Parliament might well also mean a multi-party government: an open coalition in which priorities would have to be bargained over and presented, not disputed between different factions behind closed doors as in the closed coalitions of Conservatives and Labour. Liberal Democrats also propose a number of accompanying changes in parliamentary procedure: a stronger role for parliamentary committees, with the time and the expertise to examine issues and to consider new laws in detail before they are put before the whole House; a fundamental restructuring of ministerial Question Time to make it less confrontational and more informative; parliamentary scrutiny of all agencies that spend public money. Fewer ministers in the House, with chairholders of committee given extra status and staff, would lead to a House of Commons that educated the electorate and held the government to account, rather than the government-controlled body we suffer now.

The House of Lords as it operates at present lacks the legitimacy to operate as an effective second chamber. Nearly forty years after the introduction of life peerages, its membership is still dominated by members who have inherited their seats: the products of state patronage a century or more ago, even less easy to defend than state patronage today. There is a useful role for a second chamber, differently constituted from the Commons, to play: to provide a second opinion on proposed laws passed by a busier and more partisan House of Commons, to examine specialized questions through its committees and to direct the government's attention to neglected issues through its debates. The built-in Conservative majority of hereditary peers at present undermines the Lords' credibility in acting as a constructive critic to an alternative government. As an immediate step the automatic right of hereditary peers to attend must be ended and the secretive process of appointing life peers made more transparent. As part of our overall programme of constitutional reform we would then move towards a democratic second chamber (a Senate), two thirds of whom will be elected from broad constituencies in Scotland, Wales and the regions of England, and one third nominated by a joint committee of both Houses so as to bring in independent persons with a wide range of experience and expertise.

Citizens' rights in Britain are protected by Parliament – *unless* Parliament votes to override them, or fails to check government actions which trample on them. Successive British governments insisted that *other* countries' constitutions needed written guarantees. Here in Britain, it was asserted, the underlying decency and gentlemanly behaviour of English parliamentarians was enough. British political leaders took an active role in launching the European Convention on Human Rights in 1950, apparently assuming that it would not be needed in a 'naturally democratic' country like Britain; it has not yet been incorporated into United Kingdom law.

The 1689 Bill of Rights has been occasionally cited as all that Britain needs – apart from the Magna Carta of 1216 – as a basic constitutional document. That declaration entrenches parliamentary supremacy. It was, incidentally, amended by the

Conservative majority in Parliament in 1995, redefining 'parliamentary privilege' in order to allow Neil Hamilton MP to sue the *Guardian* for libel – a Conservative constitutional change undertaken to suit short-term Conservative interests. In recent years more and more British cases have followed the long and expensive path to the European Court of Human Rights in Strasbourg. It has ruled amongst many other cases on the weakness of safeguards for personal privacy in police telephone tapping, on restrictions on prisoners' correspondence and visits, on use of the law of contempt of court to limit free expression, on judicial protection for mental patients, on solitary confinement in prison.

We want to incorporate a written statement of individual citizens' rights, enforceable by the courts against government as well as against powerful private interests, into a written constitution. We propose to use the European Convention of Human Rights as the basis for such a document. Beyond this, we want to replace the Official Secrets Act (introduced as a 'temporary' measure before the First World War, and last revised by the Conservatives in 1989) with a Freedom of Information Act, to spell out the detail of citizens' rights of access to official information, covering both factual documents and policy advice. It would also give each citizen right of access to information which government held about her or him – increasingly important as government computers store and cross-reference information on individuals.

We would reinforce the position of the Parliamentary Commissioner for Administration (the Ombudsman) as a source of redress for individuals with complaints against administrative decisions. We would further strengthen citizens' rights to obtain review through the courts. Government should be forced to provide satisfactory reasons for administrative decisions and to provide the courts with relevant information when challenged, not hide behind claims to 'public-interest immunity' as it did in the Matrix Churchill case over arms sales to Iraq. At the same time the recruitment and appointment of judges needs to be reformed, replacing the present secret and government-controlled process with a public judicial services commission, and replacing the present Judicial Committee of the House of Lords with a supreme court whose members would be nominated by the judicial services commission and approved by the appropriate committee of the House of Commons.

Every other democratic country has institutions and procedures to regulate the potentially arbitrary behaviour of government, controls which are stronger than those in Britain. British governments have argued that such written rules and procedures are not needed here; the British Parliament can be trusted by its citizens, unlike foreign parliaments and governments where – as Michael Portillo famously remarked – influence can be bought and governments bend the rules. But the last ten years in Britain have given us all overwhelming evidence that our own Parliament cannot be trusted either; that influence is actively bought and sold; and that government is repeatedly engaged in bending its own rules. We need the new constitutional settlement which I have set out, for all these reasons. We need a Parliament freed from government domination, more representative in its composition, contained within a framework of rules which can be tested in the courts and which can be amended only by an exceptional majority of both houses, ratified by popular referendum.

Spreading power

One of the most striking developments in British government over the past twenty years has been the reduction of local democracy. Conservative central government has made a determined effort to limit the ability of Britain's regions and communities to resist nationally imposed changes. Metropolitan Councils and the Greater London Council were abolished, other local authorities reorganized and their boundaries redrawn; some authorities were reorganized and reshaped again in 1995–6. The Poll Tax was intended both to limit the ability of local councils to raise local taxes and to drive transient young people and the unemployed off the electoral register. Its replacement by the Council Tax has left local government overwhelmingly dependent on national government for the money needed to carry out its tasks. In 1979 local authorities raised half of their expenditure from local taxation. In 1995 they were able to raise themselves only £1 in every £5 that they spent; for the remainder they were dependent on grants from central government, assessed according to changing political criteria in which central funding has poured into the Conservatives' flagship authorities of Westminster and Wandsworth at the expense of Liberal Democrat/Labour Lambeth and Labour-run Sheffield.

Conservatives insist that local government exists only by permission of Parliament, to be changed or further limited whenever the government carries through Parliament some new regulation. They also claim that the United Kingdom is too small to disperse power from the centre: that the people in Whitehall, in effect, know best how to direct schools, nurseries, hospitals and nursing homes, to regulate street cleaning and lighting, policing and parking, home helps and meals on wheels. It is a minimalist view of democracy, and a maximalist view of what Parliament and central government alone can manage; a short trip to the Netherlands or Denmark would have shown ministers that countries much smaller than Britain manage much better with provincial and local government. The Conservative press – the London-based *Daily Mail* in particular – has built up a caricature of local democracy, picking out a handful of corrupt Labour-dominated local authorities as representative of the whole, while treating far more gently the behaviour of the appointed bodies which have taken over their functions. An all-party report from a House of Lords committee in 1996 warned that Britain is now approaching the point at which local government could 'just be abolished by a tough central administration with a solid parliamentary majority'.

In place of elected regional and local government the Conservatives have created a network of centrally appointed committees: over 5,000 non-elected bodies carrying out executive functions on behalf of the government, responsible for a large proportion of government expenditure and paying some of their appointees large salaries. Andrew Marr of the *Independent* reports that there have been more than 150 Acts of Parliament since 1979 cutting back on the powers of local authorities, and that the appointed bodies to which powers have been transferred now spend £24 billion of public money a year. This is a new system of local rule from the centre, by people whom the central government trusts and therefore pays. This government has appointed Conservative supporters without regard for local preferences – most scandalously in Wales. They would presumably be replaced by a different government when power changes, with an over-representation of trade unionists instead of businessmen – unless this essentially corrupt system is itself changed.

At the regional level, too, there is administration without accountability, under central government control, largely unreported to Parliament. The situation is at its most extreme in Scotland. A separate nation with a separate legal system is governed by the Secretary of State for Scotland as a Conservative viceroy, with only a weak Commons committee to hold him to account. Under him the Scottish Office has responsibilities (for health, education, fisheries, transport and planning) which range across those of several English ministerial departments. Wales has its own Welsh Office, directed by a succession of English Secretaries of State – a reflection of the inability of the Conservatives to find competent ministers from among their six Welsh MPs. But also in the English regions – in Leeds, Manchester, Newcastle, Bristol, Birmingham and Nottingham, and Guildford – the Conservatives re-established in 1993 a regional level of administrative government: 'Integrated Regional Offices' of six national ministries, pulling together the different dimensions of national policy at regional level but without any public debate or democratic regional input.

The Conservatives have compensated by giving national ministers regional labels. There is, for example, a 'minister for London'; in the summer of 1996 another was publicly declared to be acting as 'minister for the south-west'. Government has to be carried out at regional and local levels; it *is* carried out – in Britain as on the European continent and in North America. But here, unlike in other countries, it is conducted by appointed bodies and officials without democratic discussion or control.

The sense of grievance at centralized London control is felt most strongly in Scotland and Wales. The creation of an elected Scottish Parliament, and of a Welsh Senedd, would not involve any vast administrative changes; the administration is already there, under the control of London ministers. Liberal Democrats and our historical predecessors, the Liberals, have supported the right of the Scots and Welsh (and the Irish) to democratic self-government for over a hundred years. Conservative insistence that London always knows best provoked Ireland's secession. Another period of Conservative government in Britain, in which a majority heavily dependent on south-east England imposed detailed laws on Scotland, would risk a surge of support for independence in Scotland as well. A more democratic election system must ensure that the injustice of long periods of single-party rule from London, based upon a minority of the popular vote, is not replaced by long periods of single-party rule in Wales and Scotland. The relationship between these autonomous governments and London will then develop through practice and political negotiation – as in other democratic countries. A United Kingdom second chamber which was elected on the basis of national constituencies in Scotland and Northern Ireland and Wales, and regional constituencies in England, would help to mediate between the two levels.

Within England we want to restore immediately an elected regional authority for London, and bring together representatives of local authorities at regional level in the first instance to oversee regional development plans and to take back from appointed bodies the supervision of regional administration and spending. We would encourage English regions to move on from there to elected assemblies, since we believe that their usefulness as a focus for regional priorities and a complement to local and national government would become clear. Such an extension of democracy would also open up patterns of recruitment to political leadership, now so narrowly pursued through the British Parliament. In the USA and Germany, in the Netherlands and Spain, potential national leaders make their reputations and establish bonds of trust with voters as often through city or regional government as through national government – providing a much larger pool of talent and experience on which governments can draw. We will expect and allow these regional authorities to have direct links with the European Union and with regional authorities in neighbouring countries. South-east England has issues to discuss with northern France which do not need always to go through central government in London and Paris. Scotland has interests to represent in Brussels which its representatives should be able to explain for themselves.

Northern Ireland is a more complicated region – or half-nation. It was for fifty years the only part of the United Kingdom to be allowed its own regional parliament (at Stormont), partly because the Conservatives who held power at Westminster during most of those years were confident that its majority would remain Conservative and Unionist. Consent then broke down between the majority and minority communities in Northern Ireland, the determined assertion of privilege by the majority countered by systematic aggression from among the minority – and Stormont was abolished. Liberal Democrats have welcomed the Anglo-Irish Agreement, which provides for the people of Northern Ireland to negotiate their own future through institutions designed to represent as far as possible the different shades of opinion in the province. We have pressed for guarantees of equal citizenship through a Bill of Rights, and see the devolution of powers to a new power-sharing assembly as a constructive move in rebuilding popular consent. Long-term stability and rebuilt consent clearly require the involvement of an international level as well – as is evident in the active partnership between the British and Irish governments. A looser United Kingdom, with cross-border cooperation accepted and encouraged within the

European Union, is part of the answer to a conflict embedded in old doctrines of sovereignty and supremacy and exclusive national identities.

The revival of local government is a necessary part of the process of reviving the pride and the local enterprise of communities throughout Britain. The great city and county councils of a hundred years ago shaped Britain's communities, leaving us a legacy of colleges and universities, libraries, museums, theatres, art galleries, parks, public spaces and public buildings from which we still benefit. We will return responsibilities and financial autonomy to local authorities, from central government and from non-elected bodies. A more democratic voting system – proportional representation – will guard against the re-emergence of single-party control over long periods, which allowed the growth of corruption in some Labour and Conservative-held Councils. Where Liberal Democrats control local councils we have already encouraged the growth of parish and town councils within local authority areas, to involve people within communities in considering and making local choices. Local authorities and regional governments work in partnership in other European countries; our aim is to build similar partnerships within Britain. John Stuart Mill's principle of 'the greatest dissemination of power consistent with efficiency' is still valid. Power, like wealth, needs to be spread as widely as possible to create the open, self-confident civil society which Liberal Democrats want.

Nation and state, subject and citizen

What makes you proud to be British? What do you think of as the best qualities of the British character, the best elements in Britain's historical tradition which we should hope to pass on to our children? The argument over the reshaping of Britain's constitution comes close to the question of Britain's national identity, as also to that of Britain's relations with the rest of Europe.

Britain (or rather, England) contests with Iceland and Switzerland the claim to be the world's oldest continuously operating democracy. The national myths of all three countries look back to deliberative assemblies in the Middle Ages. The Swiss and Icelandic claims rest on firmer ground than the English; their primitive parliaments assembled all the adult men who could attend, whereas the English Parliament was a gathering of nobles and bishops, and representatives of the towns and counties. The modern British parliamentary tradition, like the Palace of Westminster itself, is a nineteenth-century creation with idealized medieval elements in its design.

The extension of these nineteenth-century liberal institutions into a modern mass democracy proceeded in Britain in parallel with the similar establishment of democratic institutions across the Atlantic and the English Channel: in France, the Netherlands and Belgium, Denmark and Sweden. When in the Second World War all except Sweden collapsed under German attack, the United Kingdom remained the defender of European liberal democracy, protected from invasion by the English Channel and by American supplies. Wartime propaganda reinforced the Anglo-Saxon myth of an England that was naturally free – of free men and free institutions, coming down from Saxon times – facing a naturally unfree continent. Refugees from that unfree continent embraced in their turn the myth of Anglo-Saxon liberty, writing admiring historical studies of the English Parliament and 'gentry', and preaching the doctrines of English free trade. British sovereignty and British identity were wrapped up in the idea of a sovereign Parliament, the symbol of a free Britain.

After the Second World War those who returned to rebuild democracy on the continent looked to Britain to provide a lead in building international institutions through which European states and citizens could work together. They hoped that this would extend democratic participation under British leadership to the European level. They found to their disappointment that English political leaders were lost in the complacent superiority of their own national myth. The idealization of Westminster as the 'mother of Parliaments', incapable of improvement, still echoes in the constitutional rhetoric of John Major and Michael Portillo, as in the anti-European rhetoric of John Redwood and Michael Howard. Devolution to Scotland and Wales, Kenneth Clarke argued last year, would 'diminish the United Kingdom' in Europe and the world.

Anti-Europeans and constitutional traditionalists, in both the Conservative and Labour parties, cling to an outdated idea of British identity. Liberal Democrats prefer to reinterpret national identity to fit our now-diverse society, as we work to build stronger democratic institutions. For us the best elements in the British tradition are those of toleration and dissent, of citizens protesting against arbitrary state power, of an eighteenth-century Parliament which successfully resisted the growth of state patronage, of a nineteenth-century Parliament which permitted and encouraged the growth of a lively local democracy. We want to pass on to our children a democratic tradition of which we can really be proud. But that *requires* constitutional reform.

FOUR

The Wealth of the Nation

The wealth of the nation lies in the skills of its people and their ability to work together, in the stock of public and private investment it has accumulated, the natural resources within its territory and the quality of its natural and built environment. Good economic management husbands those resources: reinvesting as they are depleted, renewing skills for each new generation, caring for and maintaining those resources which are non-renewable. Economic management is not therefore just a matter of short-term adjustment – of raising or lowering interest rates and taxes, of juggling with incentives and regulations. Long-term economic management transfers wealth between generations: wisely building up public resources, or foolishly depleting them. Sustainable economic development requires a redefinition of conventional measures of economic growth, and a careful balance between openness to rapid change and innovation on the one hand and concern for its impact on society and on the environment on the other.

The British economy is now undergoing rapid and massive change – as is the wider global economy. The 'creative destruction' of technological change has demolished the heavy industries which provided mass employment, leaving space for new industries and services to emerge. More new jobs were created in Western Europe between 1975 and 1995 than in the postwar years of economic recovery and full employment between 1950 and 1970; but unemployment nevertheless rose sharply, as steelworks and coalmines closed, as textile mills and clothing factories modernized or shifted production abroad, and as the electronic revolution cut a swathe through offices and state administrations. Britain adjusted less well than its competitors in the 1970s, investing too little and disguising painful adjustment through inflation. Economic adjustment in the 1980s and 1990s has been more successful. But the strategy adopted has run down investment further while fuelling consumption. It has encouraged wage cuts for less-skilled workers while allowing top salaries to soar.

The key question for British economic policy is how to make the best of our specific national advantages in a global market which severely limits any government's freedom of action. British governments can no longer control the instruments of national economic management without close cooperation with others. British interest rates are directly affected by Bundesbank decisions; British exports rise and fall with economic growth and spending in our most important partners, in Western Europe and North America. Old notions of economic nationalism – of reasserting Britain's economic and monetary sovereignty – simply have no relevance to our country's present position. One of the central contradictions of Thatcherite policy has been between its reassertion of national independence and its determined pursuit of inward investment by foreign companies as the vehicle for economic regeneration.

Effective economic management requires active cooperation with other governments – which means in the first place European governments. Successful British companies now regard Britain as their base and Europe as their home market. For most major British companies the European market accounts for the greater part of their sales and production, and for the supply of the components and raw materials on which they depend. That is why Liberal Democrats – like leading members of the Confederation of British Industry and the Chambers of Commerce – believe that it is in Britain's interest to join a single European currency as and when it goes ahead. Britain has no alternative to some form of European economic integration. We should therefore seek to influence the direction of shared European policies, not opt out bad-temperedly from the game.

John Major has spoken of an 'Asian–US alternative' to the European economic model, reflecting romantic ideas on the Conservative Right that Britain might do better to link itself to the fast-growing economies of East Asia and the friendly free traders of North America. In reality there are enormous differences between Japanese, Chinese, Korean and South-East Asian approaches to markets and growth and that of the USA. Government has played an active developmental role in all Asian economies, an authoritarian role in most, with protection from foreign competition and access to cheap capital for favoured industries. Social networks, a strong sense of family and of shared community, and high public and private investment in education have also strengthened the foundations of Asian economic growth.

The USA, in contrast, has suffered from social breakdown in its cities and rising inequality of incomes in its pursuit of a free market, successfully creating millions of new jobs as workers moved across the American continent, but without achieving anything like an Asian rate of economic growth. Like Britain, and in sharp contrast to East Asia, it has suffered from a structural deficit in foreign trade; like Britain, the deliberate encouragement of greater inequality through taxation policy has failed to produce the promised flowering of private enterprise. The German economy, the core of the European model, is itself undergoing major changes as the costs of integrating the former East Germany weigh West German taxpayers down. Intelligent British policy-makers need to learn from all these examples, while recognizing that the model we follow must be designed to match Britain's particular circumstances and needs.

The successful economies of the world – as a succession of studies have shown – share a number of characteristics. They put the highest priority on education and training, recognizing that quality products and quality service depend upon a quality workforce. They have a culture of long-term investment, of adaptable labour markets, of strong internal competition and a dynamic small-business sector. And they rest on a firm basis of social integration, rather than on the adversarial and aggressive capitalism found in America and Britain.

Over the past generation British citizens have consumed too much and invested too little. Improvements in health care and a declining birthrate have increased the proportion of retired people, and reduced the proportion of those in work. It is vital to the long-term future of our economy to raise levels of saving, of both public and private investment. It is also essential to the long-term cohesion of our society to maintain appropriate public and private social provision. Governments *can* cut taxes by shifting obligations from the public to the private sector. But five pence off income tax, for example, offset by compulsory private health insurance and larger private pension provisions might well leave the majority of people much worse off. Responsible economic management must set out these choices for the electorate, while arguing strongly for sustainable economic policies and for a shift from consumption to investment.

What hinders Britain

In the 1970s Britain was held back, amongst other economic weaknesses, by the inflexibility of our labour force, clinging to trade union habits and working practices which derived their shape from industrial conflicts in the years before and after the First World War. Mrs Thatcher's government was determined to break trade union resistance to change, and succeeded in doing so. But in the process it destroyed much of Britain's manufacturing base. The monetary squeeze on the economy between 1980 and 1982 saw the pound's value rise by a third against other currencies. Many British companies had gone bankrupt, many foreign companies closed their British factories, before the pound fell back again.

The two greatest constraints on British economic growth for the previous thirty years had been the shortage of manufacturing capacity, which led to a rise in imports and a yawning trade deficit every time domestic economic growth took off, and the shortage of skilled labour – which led to a competition among employers every time the economy grew and therefore to another burst of wage inflation. The boom and bust, stop and go cycles of British economic policy followed from these structural shortages. Mrs Thatcher's monetary squeeze left Britain even shorter of industrial capacity, while her government's squeeze on education spending has meant that the skills needed to staff expanding industries remain in scarce supply.

Inward investment has partly rebuilt British industry, and is now contributing to the reduction of Britain's trade deficit. British-built Nissans are now exported to Belgium and Germany, British-assembled Samsung TVs and NEC microwaves to continental markets. But Britain remains more dependent on services for employment and for economic growth – from banking and insurance through supermarkets to tourism – than almost any other advanced industrial country. We have some of the world's leading service sector companies, in British Airways and British Telecom. But even the overseas earnings of such expanding British-based companies have failed to compensate for the weakened industrial base. There remains a worrying deficit in Britain's balance of payments.

The dominant financial culture which Thatcherite ideology supported and reinforced has also held Britain back. Companies have been pressed to maintain high dividends rather than to reinvest or pursue longer-term strategies. The City of London has focused on annual, even six-monthly, company results rather than on prospects for long-term growth. Banks have invested in international operations far more than in support for small and medium-sized British companies. Insurance companies, pension funds and unit trusts – in Britain as in the USA – have competed with each other in pursuing short-term profits with funds which investors have placed with them for ten to twenty-five years or longer.

Corporate predators, from Lord Hanson to Sir James Goldsmith, have prowled after the shares of companies which did not reflect underlying value, with merchant banks competing to profit from the fees which takeover bids provide; forcing companies to place a higher value on immediate profitability than on long-term viability, to prefer the economies of 'restructuring' (job cuts and sell-offs) to the potential of research and development or of reinvestment of profits in new equipment or additional capacity. In many cases, it has thus become more 'rational' for British companies to shrink than to expand, to return funds to shareholders than to invest. It is part of the paradox of contemporary Britain that foreign-owned companies in Britain – fortunately – pursue longer-term strategies than their British counterparts. It is all the more paradoxical that the quality of their management is still acknowledged to be superior to that of many of their British counterparts, but that the salaries their senior executives receive are often lower.

Conservative ideology twisted Britain's economy further by cutting back on support for civilian research and development, while actively supporting military industry. Free-market principles were proclaimed to justify a sharp reduction in support for regional industrial regeneration, leaving the English regions and the other nations of the UK to rely very heavily on funds provided through European Union regional programmes. Defence industry, in contrast, has been fostered through government contracts, supported through government-funded research, and promoted through ministerial and prime ministerial interventions with foreign governments which were potential customers. Arms contracts with Malaysia, with Iraq, with Oman and with Saudi Arabia have – in different ways and to differing extents – involved distortions in normal rules of government-to-government and government–company relations. Too large a proportion of Britain's home-owned manufacturing capacity has thus become dependent on arms sales, at a time when the world armaments market is shrinking sharply.

The combination of these factors has left Britain with one of the lowest levels of investment in plant and equipment in the industrial world. We have been forced to depend on devaluation and low wages to attract inward investment, with a much smaller small-company sector than most of our competitor countries. Despite a succession of training initiatives, it remained the case in 1994 that only 55 per cent of seventeen-year-olds in Britain were in full-time education or training, compared with 93 per cent in Germany and 87 per cent in France.

Government preoccupation with privatization has invested public funds in fees for consultants rather than in renewing Britain's stock of investment. It has led, for example, to a sharp reduction in Britain's capacity to build railway equipment and stock as orders have dried up: leaving a predicted post-privatization surge in investment in trains and trams to pull in imports for lack of capacity at home. The promise that privatization would increase investment in industries previously hobbled by public accounting rules has been a disappointment. Investment in the water industry, in particular, has risen little, while charges, salaries and profits have soared.

Britain's economy has suffered over the past fifty years from too many twists and turns in government policy, as ministers change and governments subordinate economic strategy to pre-election political needs. The 1992 election repeated the cycle, with tax cuts beforehand and increases afterwards. 'Much the most important explanation of the differences in income across countries,' Professor Mancur Olson noted in a recent comparative study of economic development, 'is the difference in their economic policies and institutions.' The inadequacy of Britain's political institutions and the incoherent and rapidly changing economic policies which they have permitted have also held Britain back.

What government can do

In an open, increasingly global economy there are limits to what any government can do on its own to manage its domestic economy. But there remain nevertheless a number of ways in which active government can improve the competitive position of its economy in the global market. The Liberal Democrat economic strategy aims to create the conditions under which an effective partnership between government and private enterprise can rebuild, renew and revitalize the British economy to compete effectively under conditions of rapid global change.

The primary requirement is to increase investment:

- higher investment in people through better education and training;

- higher investment in industry through a stable fiscal and monetary framework, through a shift in the balance of taxation, through changes in the structure of company law and in the obligations of pension fund trustees;

- higher public investment through changes in public accounting rules and through a more effective partnership between public authorities and private funds; and

- higher investment in innovation through encouraging small enterprises in new fields.

A sound framework of competition policy and market regulation is also needed, to encourage producers to innovate and to control costs, and to set out clear rules for privatized utilities. A shift in the balance of taxation away from employment towards energy use and resource depletion will create new jobs, stimulate investment in environmental technology and move towards a more sustainable long-term framework for Britain's economy. The remaining sections of this chapter set out some of these proposals in more detail.

The political reforms which Liberal Democrats propose will provide Britain with a more stable foundation for economic policy, through reducing the ability of any single party to manipulate interest rates and taxes for short-term ends. We would in addition transform the Bank of England into a UK reserve bank, with day-to-day independence. Its policy-making council would include representatives of the nations and regions of the UK alongside its senior executives; their appointment would be subject to the approval of the House of Commons Treasury Select Committee, to which the Governor would report half-yearly, with full parliamentary debates on the conduct of monetary policy as necessary. The objectives of monetary policy would be defined in a published agreement between the Bank's Governor and the Chancellor of the Exchequer.

A stable framework of European policy will also encourage investment. Given that the British economy is now increasingly integrated into the broader European economy, with companies based in Britain operating across the European market, it is in Britain's clear long-term interests to cooperate with our partners in strengthening Europe's competitive position. Liberal Democrats are persuaded that it is in Britain's interest to work with other EU members to achieve a workable monetary union. We share the views of the Chancellor of the Exchequer, Kenneth Clarke, that Britain has little to fear from inclusion and risks many disadvantages from exclusion – most of all for Britain's financial services – and regret that so many others within the Conservative government disagree with him. We do not share the views of Robin Cook and others in the Labour Party that Britain would benefit from retaining the option of devaluation. Countries with weak currencies have to maintain higher interest rates to compensate, which means paying more out of tax revenue in interest on government debt. A saving of $1\frac{1}{2}$ per cent in government interest rates, as a consequence of joining a single currency, would be worth £8 billion – available for investment elsewhere – over five years.

The details of monetary union are still under negotiation. It is vital that Britain play an active role in negotiating those details, and in shaping the new institutions. The negotiations so far have pushed governments in France, Germany and Italy towards needed liberalization of markets and reductions in state control and subsidies – all developments which bring them closer to the model of a European economy which suits Britain best. Elimination of exchange rate volatility and the transaction costs of currency exchanges within the European market would be of particular help to smaller businesses in exporting to the continent, and would give companies large and small the confidence to invest to supply that market at predictable prices. Participation in the single currency from the outset is also important to the international competitiveness of Britain's financial services sector, in particular to the City of London in maintaining its position as a key financial centre for the European region.

Liberal Democrats therefore see clear potential benefits to Britain of entry into monetary union from the beginning. Participation in launching the single currency will also ensure that Britain influences the direction of European monetary and economic policies. Too often over the past fifty years, Britain has joined in common policies after others have launched them, with the framework already designed to fit the interests of the first members. We should not repeat that error.

The positive role of public finance

Taxation and public finance are among the key issues in British politics, on which the intelligent voter should expect an honest answer, not evasion. Sadly, debate on these subjects has become more and more dishonest, with newspapers campaigning at the same time for tax cuts and for improved public services and too many politicians pretending that they can promise the public both. President Reagan's administration in the USA pursued the strategy which John Redwood, the *Daily Mail* and *The Times* call for in Britain: cuts in taxation now, intended to force cuts in services later. The American experience, however, was disastrous. Cuts in Medicare and in social security proved much harder to achieve than Reaganites had promised; right-wing determination to raise defence spending widened the deficit further. The USA has been left with a mountain of public debt, which the next generation of taxpayers will be forced to repay.

Irresponsibility and dishonesty in public financing, thankfully, have not yet reached comparable levels in Britain. Economic commentators have, however, expressed growing concern about the widening gap between revenue and expenditure, and the collapse in public investment, over the past two years. The use of receipts from selling off capital assets – privatization – to fund current spending has been compounded by a rise in borrowing. 'Public investment,' the Coopers and Lybrand *UK Economic Outlook* for June 1996 noted, 'fell away dramatically in 1995 as the Government cut its spending to leave room for the tax cuts it introduced' – contributing to a sharp recession in the construction sector in 1995–6. The Private Finance Initiative (PFI), which was intended to take the place of such public investment, has so far disappointed even its strongest promoters. The PFI operates by postponing the burden of public investment, imposing it on future users through recurrent charges. As the *Economist* commented in June 1996, 'it allows projects to be bought now and paid for later' – adding that 'suspicion of the PFI as a politicians' fiddle is still justified'.

Paddy Ashdown has pledged the Liberal Democrats to open up the closed Treasury world of taxation and spending, and set out to the public what it is possible to afford for different levels of taxation and what it is not: no taxation without explanation. Liberal Democrat proposals to increase spending on education come with a maximum cost attached: an extra penny on income tax will pay for the programme. Our proposals on health spending have similarly been linked to an increase in tobacco taxation and to closure of loopholes in executive benefits.

The decline of public trust in politicians over the past two decades is closely related to mistrust of taxation, combined with lack of understanding of the constraints on public spending. We will reform the budget process to include a report from the government to taxpayers on how it has spent their money over the past year – an obligation which the Conservatives have imposed on local government but not on themselves while in power. We favour extension of the principle that specific revenues be attached to specific expenditure where possible – 'hypotheca-tion', in the language of tax experts – as a means of rebuilding public trust in public finance. Thus experiments in road charging, for instance, should be used to fund improvements in urban public transport, as airport taxes are already allocated to the maintenance and improvement of surface access.

Sound finance was one of the principles around which Gladstone built the Liberal Party, in opposition to the unsound borrowing and spending of nineteenth-century Conservatives. Liberal Democrats today insist on the same principle against such unsound practices as presenting cuts in income tax (recouped by rises in indirect taxes) as cuts in overall taxation. The golden rule of public finance is that governments should only borrow to invest for the long term and to smooth out the peaks and troughs of economic cycles – generating a surplus when growth picks up to repay deficits incurred during periods of recession. The Conservatives have broken that golden rule, both during the period before the 1992 election and again in 1995–6.

Liberal Democrats will alter public accounting rules to distinguish much more clearly between current and capital receipts and spending, to show the rate of depletion of public capital assets and of investment to replace or maintain them. We will also build into these accounts estimated projections of future obligations incurred, both in terms of PFI charges and of predicted state pension obligations.

So Liberal Democrats do not promise to reduce the overall burden of taxation. The Conservatives have failed, in spite of their repeated promises, to do so over the last twenty years. The demographic constraints noted in Chapter Two bear down on any British government, as an ageing population places heavier demands on the health and social security budgets. To raise levels of skill across the entire population – an essential part of any enlightened economic strategy – implies an increase in education spending rather than a cut. Health, social security and education together account for two thirds of government spending; add to that defence, police, justice, foreign relations, support for public transport, for civilian research and development, for regional regeneration, local government and local enterprise, and the search for significant reductions without severe damage to Britain's economic interests or social fabric becomes a desperate enterprise.

Fair taxation

What Liberal Democrats *do* promise is fair taxation, underpinned by public debate on spending choices, and rigorous accounting to Parliament to minimize waste. The burden of taxation and the distribution of benefits should reflect the principles of social justice: a harshly unequal society is a sharply divided society. The balance of taxation and benefits also affects individual and corporate behaviour. Taxation is therefore a powerful lever to shift behaviour towards preferred social and economic objectives.

Levels of inequality have risen more sharply in Britain in the past decade than in any other country except New Zealand. Between 1979 and 1993 the top 10 per cent of Britain's population increased their average net income by 60 per cent, while the net income of the bottom 10 per cent *fell* by 17 per cent. The Conservative promise was that acceptance of greater inequality would generate a surge of private enterprise and a rapid increase in economic growth. It has generated instead a surge in crime from a growing underclass of the unskilled and unemployed, without a stake in the society which they attack. The record of Ireland over the same period offers a striking comparison. Heavy investment in education there has been accompanied by a *reduction* in overall inequality of income, contributing to a growth rate almost double that of Britain.

Liberal Democrats are committed to raise income tax on high incomes – over £100,000 per year – to 50 per cent, and to close down tax loopholes which enable the already well-paid to profit further through profit-related pay and massive private pension contributions. Britain's wealthy carry obligations to their society in return for the opportunities they pursue within it; fair taxation is part of those obligations.

Paying for public services

There are hard choices to be made about the balance between public and private provision in welfare and services, and about the relative merits of free or subsidized provision and market charging. In health and education there is considerable evidence that state provision not only carries important social values but also provides better quality for equivalent cost. The United States spends almost as much on health from public funds as Britain, through Medicare and veterans' programmes which do not benefit a large proportion of its citizens – and spends as much again on private medicine, without achieving higher standards of health or life expectancy. Continental schemes for compulsory health insurance also carry heavier administrative overheads, and are less effective at containing costs.

'The state as monopoly employer of teachers, doctors and nurses,' Sam Brittan remarked in the *Financial Times* in August 1996, 'is pretty effective in holding down costs' – as it also is in bargaining with drugs companies and equipment suppliers. Conservative moves to promote an 'artificial market' within the NHS have led to a sharp increase in numbers of administrators and accountants employed, and a reduction in nursing and medical staff. We will promote an informed public debate about the scope for reducing budgetary burdens, by charging those in employment for aspects of – for example – hospital accommodation and higher education; we *have* to examine all possible ways of increasing the resources available. But our starting-point is that high-quality services should be available to all.

Encouraging saving, taxing pollution

The British economy still suffers from a bias towards consumption and a low rate of saving – reinforced by the tendency of governments to promote consumer booms in periods before elections. Liberal Democrats propose to encourage higher saving through introducing a National Savings 'Save As You Earn' scheme, to encourage all employees to save on a regular basis, thus broadening the incentives currently provided through the more limited TESSAs and PEPs. We plan to replace the unsatisfactory SERPs scheme for occupational pensions with obligatory personal pension plans, jointly funded by employers and employees, which would add a further six million people to the number saving towards their own pensions and make a very considerable difference to the savings rate. The proposals recently outlined by the independently minded Labour MP, Frank Field, are close to Liberal Democrat policy. There is room for public debate and, we hope, inter-party agreement on the way forward.

Taxation should aim also to encourage desired objectives, such as higher employment, and to discourage such undesirable outputs of economic activity as pollution and depletion of natural resources. A number of proposals have been floated in recent years by independent experts and international organizations to shift the burden of taxation from jobs to environmental depletion. The Conservative government has itself taken a small step in this direction, by introducing a landfill tax to encourage recycling and discourage the dumping of waste, and by introducing a modest 'fuel-tax escalator' intended to raise the real costs of petrol over a period of years.

Liberal Democrats propose a much more determined shift away from taxation on employment (through employers' National Insurance contributions) towards taxes on environmental depletion – on the carbon content of fuels, on quarrying and exploitation of natural resources – together with increases in the road-fuel escalator and the landfill tax. A 1996 study for Cambridge Econometrics of Liberal Democrat proposals for environmental tax reform (together with the similar proposals recently published by the Institute for Public Policy Research) concluded that such a shift would reduce carbon dioxide emissions by 17 per cent over the next ten years, while generating a net increase of half a million jobs – without changing the overall proportion of taxation in national income.

The encouragement such a change in relative prices would

provide to industry to substitute labour for other inputs also makes it likely that the majority of the new jobs created would be full-time and likely to attract male applicants, while lower employment costs would also boost employment in health and education. 'There are also gains,' the study concludes, 'arising from an increase in income tax (due to higher employment) and a reduction in benefits associated with unemployment.' Active government, setting a framework in which market behaviour promotes socially desired objectives and environmental sustainability: that is the Liberal Democrat approach.

Investing in people

Education plays a vital role both in economic competitiveness and in social cohesion. Liberal Democrats insist on priority investment in education, from childhood through to retirement, as essential to maintain an open society and a competitive economy for the coming generation. We are prepared to increase public spending on education in order to achieve these aims.

Our top priorities for additional resources are in pre-school and primary provision. Education from the outset teaches children to relate to each other and to learn. We will provide education for all three- and four-year-olds whose parents want it. Small children need active help from teachers to learn – and, in some cases, to learn how to behave. We therefore intend to increase the number of primary teachers, to ensure that within five years no primary school class has more than thirty pupils. Too many primary school children are being taught in huts, mobile classrooms and unsafe buildings; cuts in public expenditure have left a huge backlog in maintenance. To help kickstart the necessary programme of repairs, we would make a £500 million investment in capital expenditure.

The extension of central government control over education risks stifling experiment and originality. We would replace the current detailed National Curriculum with a Minimum Curriculum Entitlement (MCE), which all schools, state, voluntary and independent, would provide. The MCE would set basic requirements in written and spoken English, maths, science, citizenship and information technology. At the secondary level – and, as resources permit, also in the final years of primary education – children would learn a foreign language, a necessary skill in a competitive world. We attach particular importance to encouraging a broader curriculum, in which all secondary pupils will study maths and science as well as arts and the humanities to equip them for a world in which science and technology will be increasingly important. We welcome Sir Ron Dearing's proposals for a framework of post-fourteen qualifications, which were close to previous Liberal Democrat recommendations. Like him, we wish to develop a broader secondary National Certificate which will comprise components of the current GCSEs, GNVQs and A Levels. The unified qualifications system proposed and the individual Record of Achievement should ease the transition to tertiary education and the continuation of education throughout adult life.

Teachers have been battered by years of Conservative criticism, and squeezed by declining real pay. We will rebuild respect and professional standards by establishing a General Teaching Council to monitor the profession. Extra resources for education are pledged first to expand the numbers of teachers, thus relieving stress and providing greater opportunities for professional training and development. We will reform the salary structure to reflect special skills and responsibilities, and – as far as resources permit – will raise initial salaries to attract high-quality entrants to the profession.

We want to bring together the academic and practical aspects of secondary education as far as possible, encouraging schools to cooperate with local business and industry on work-experience schemes. We see schools as rooted in their local communities, and as bringing together the children of these communities; we aim therefore to raise the quality of state education to a level which will regain the confidence of middle-class parents, encouraging them to send their children to state schools close to their homes rather than opting out into the private sector. We will reduce central control, returning authority and budgetary flexibility to local councils in communities which schools serve. Local Education Authorities should work with schools in long-term strategic planning, including the provision of places and responses to changes in local demography.

In accordance with our commitment to local self-government we would return grant-maintained schools and city technology colleges to local authority control. As Liberals we have no intention of banning independent schools, nor of removing their charitable status to all schools. We would phase out the Assisted Places Scheme as children already at private schools complete their education, redirecting resources to improve state schools. Liberal Democrats in local government will encourage close cooperation between state and independent schools in sharing facilities and serving the local community.

Education should be a life-long process. In a rapidly changing world economy, retraining is a necessity for most people during their working lives. Further and higher education must therefore be encouraged to provide courses for the widest possible range of needs, rather than focusing primarily on post-school qualifications and degrees. Liberal Democrats propose to encourage those over eighteen to register for Individual Learning Accounts, to which government and employers would contribute. Government would provide each of these with an initial investment; employers would be encouraged to pay into the account on behalf of their employees. Students accumulating deficits on their Learning Accounts through permitted spending on course fees, living and study expenses would pay back through the National Insurance system once their earnings reached a defined level – and would also be encouraged to accumulate funds through this means to finance future studies. We would introduce an education and training levy at a rate of 2 per cent of companies' payroll, to be reduced by the amount companies spent on training of an approved quality or transfers to their employees' Learning Accounts.

We attach particular importance to encouraging all young people to continue their education beyond the age of sixteen. As schools and employers form closer links we will promote apprenticeships for school-leavers, together with extended work-experience schemes to assist the transition from school to work. Liberal Democrat proposals would guarantee all sixteen-to-nineteen-year-olds the equivalent of two days a week continuing education or training, for which employers would be expected to release them.

The proportion of eighteen-to-twenty-year-olds in full-time higher and further education has doubled over the past twenty years, transforming Britain's colleges and universities. The priority which Liberal Democrats attach to providing additional resources for pre-primary, primary and secondary education leaves little scope for easing the financial squeeze on universities; where additional funds can be found for tertiary education they must go first to vocational training and retraining to equip those out of work to return to employment. Three sections of society – government, employers and individual learners – benefit from the provision of higher education; we believe that all three should contribute to the cost. We remain committed to state funding for tuition fees up to the end of first-degree courses, while recognizing that students must now be expected to pay back a substantial part of their living costs away from home from the salaries they earn later.

We look forward to the Dearing Committee's proposals for the future organization and funding of tertiary education, in 1997. Liberal Democrats will support proposals to move away from the conventional structures of three-year degrees towards more flexible courses and credits which can accommodate changes in the subjects taught and the distinctive needs of mature and part-time students. We would use government funding to support broader courses in the tertiary sector, as more valuable in equipping most students with the skills they need as workers and citizens than the specialized academic degrees which too many universities – new as well as old – prefer.

Including everyone in economic activity

The most constructive contribution government can make to alleviating poverty and reducing inequality is to pursue policies which promote higher employment. Social division in Britain has sharpened as the proportion of women in work has risen, while the proportion of employed men has dropped. Sixty per cent of British households now contain two earners or more – the so-called 'work-rich'; one household in five is work-poor, with no earners at all. Changes in the system of taxation and benefits which raise the level of employment – such as the environmental tax reforms set out above – and encourage those on benefit to return to work thus directly reduce poverty and social exclusion. They also increase tax revenues and reduce social security costs: a method of cutting the social security budget at once more effective and more socially just than Conservative campaigns against single mothers and the long-term unemployed.

Britain's current tax and social security systems still trap marginal earners between benefits and low pay. Liberal Democrats would use additional revenue raised from a 50 per cent rate of income tax on high earners to raise the threshold at which income tax is levied. Integration of National Insurance with income tax, while raising the threshold at which National Insurance becomes payable and abolishing the top limit on National Insurance contributions, will further assist the low paid and distribute the burden of direct taxation more fairly according to ability to pay. A proportion of income tax will be designated as a 'pensions payment', earmarked to contribute to the funding of state pensions.

We will also assess benefit entitlements more flexibly, enabling people with casual jobs to claim benefit more easily during times when they are not earning. To reduce the burdens on employers, we will simplify the system of National Insurance contributions, while working towards the elimination of employers' contributions as environmental tax reforms are introduced. Our Benefit Transfer Programme will enable the long-term unemployed to have their benefits payable as a voucher to an employer prepared to offer them work, who will be required to train the new employee in return.

Abolition of wages councils has allowed some employers to reduce wages to levels where people in work remain dependent on social security subsidies to support their families. Liberal Democrats would establish regional Low Pay Commissions to agree and recommend appropriate minimum hourly rates of pay; employees paid below that level would have the right to apply to an industrial tribunal for an increase to that level, and would be protected from dismissal during the considerations of that tribunal. The publicity such a process would attract to restaurants and service providers paying below the minimum recommended levels would itself bring market pressures to bear, as consumers use the information provided to transfer their custom.

Early retirement also deprives the economy of useful activity, and adds to the burden of social security. One in three men between fifty-five and sixty-five in the UK is now not in paid work. Liberal Democrat proposals to improve opportunities for retraining for second (or third) careers and to shift taxation from labour to resource use will also increase the opportunity for men in this age group to find new jobs. The experience of firms which have recruited from this age category has demonstrated that they provide reliable labour, and that they are anxious to return to work. To encourage a higher proportion of Britain's middle-aged population to remain economically active, we want to move towards a flexible 'decade of retirement' between sixty and seventy, with incentives for those who postpone the age at which they begin to draw their pensions.

Liberal Democrats – like our Gladstonian predecessors of 150 years ago – are opposed in principle to the proliferation of tax concessions and loopholes. Taxation should be as simple and transparent as possible, benefits as efficiently targeted as possible. We would, for example, phase out Mortgage Interest Relief, creating instead a uniform mortgage benefit for all home owners and freeing resources to fund improvements in the scope and level of the targeted Housing Benefit. For the long-term unemployed, as noted above, we would expand and improve the working benefit scheme to help them back into work and retraining. We would reduce confusion and bureaucracy by combining Family Credit and Income Support into a single means-tested low-income benefit.

We would transform the Invalid Carer's Allowance into a new Carer's Benefit, to allow carers more scope to work when they can without substantial or immediate loss of benefits. For people with disabilities we would establish a new Partial Capacity Benefit, to encourage these people back into part-time work where possible. The Liberal Democrat aim is to use taxation and benefits to offer every citizen the opportunity to contribute to Britain's economy and society, and to structure the market so that market forces operate to create the virtuous circle of rising employment, rising tax revenues and parallel savings to public spending on social security.

Fostering enterprise and innovation

Higher investment and a more productive labour force will help to revitalize Britain's economy. But the UK also needs greater enterprise – the get-up-and-go to establish and run successful new businesses. It also needs a greater emphasis on investment geared to the future, to innovation and to clean technologies.

Small and medium-sized enterprises generate three quarters of all new jobs in the UK. They provide the basis for future British-based major enterprises, and meanwhile act as a competitive spur to keep large companies on their toes. Despite improvements in the provision of venture capital, however, such enterprises continue to face difficulties in securing start-up funding and finance for development. Liberal Democrats would establish vigorous codes of practice to ensure that the banks serve the small-business community better, and would extend the powers of the banking ombudsman in cases of dispute. We would legislate to make interest payable on late debts, and require such interest payments to be published in company annual reports. We would introduce an investment allowance limited to £200,000 a year per company, to give relative advantage to smaller enterprises; and we would abolish the Uniform Business Rate, returning revenues to local authorities as the basis for partnership to promote local enterprise.

Both Britain's financial institutions and Britain's structure of government are too highly centralized to respond to local and regional initiatives and small companies outside London. Germany's far stronger and technologically advanced *Mittelstand* – the layer of regionally based small and medium-sized enterprises – is supported by a partnership between regional governments, regional universities and research institutes and regional banks. Liberal Democrats would return to local and regional authorities the primary responsibility for industrial regeneration in their areas, bringing together in regional development agencies the functions of the integrated regional offices of central government in liaison with chambers of commerce, TECs and universities. We would encourage financial institutions to underwrite regional development banks, to supplement the contribution of the venture capital sector in identifying and supporting promising new firms. Over time the presence in banks and in government agencies of more people with a degree of scientific and technological awareness – as Liberal Democrat reforms of secondary and tertiary curricula take effect – will also provide a more sympathetic response to the needs of innovators and entrepreneurs.

Neither Britain's business nor financial cultures have in recent decades been friendly to long-term relationships between different stakeholders or to constructive partnerships between managers, suppliers, employees and local government. Changes in the law alone cannot change cultural attitudes; that will come gradually, we may hope, from a shift away from an adversarial political culture, from a reduction of the division between private and state education, and from a dispersal of élites currently over-concentrated in south-eastern England. But changes in corporate governance, and in the lead which government provides to financial and industrial élites, can help.

Liberal Democrats would promote a shift in business culture by requiring the publication in annual reports of expenditure on research and development and on education and training, as well as of major changes in relationships with suppliers. Companies would also be required to report more fully to their employees and to establish appropriate structures for employee consultations. Listed companies would be required to submit their remuneration committees to direct election by shareholders. Pension-fund trustees would be required, in their turn, to inform those on whose behalf they hold the funds of their policies in investment and in enforcing corporate accountability. Liberal Democrats in local government are already taking steps to use their position as trustees for council pension funds to promote intelligent and long-term company management.

Liberal Democrats see competition as a dynamic force in economic development wherever market forces allow multiple providers: competition where possible, regulation where necessary when natural monopolies exist within either the private or the public sector. We would combine the Monopolies and Mergers Commission and the Office of Fair Trading into a single Restrictive Practices Office, accountable to a parliamentary select committee. We would similarly combine the separate regulators for privatized utilities into a more authoritative Office of Utility Regulation, similarly subject to the scrutiny of a parliamentary select committee. This would ensure more open debate on regulatory choices and priorities, and greater public understanding of the issues involved.

An economy for the long term

Sound public finance, higher levels of investment and reinvestment, higher-quality education and training, all contribute to sustainable economic development. But economic development must also be sustainable in environmental terms. That requires a shift in domestic economic priorities, as well as a change of direction in British cooperation with our European partners and active engagement with them in promoting new approaches to global environmental protection.

The environmental tax reforms outlined earlier are close to proposals for European carbon taxation put forward by the European Commission, though not yet accepted by the majority of member governments. Denmark and the Netherlands have moved ahead to implement several of the proposed reforms; most expert opinion concludes that it would be to Britain's advantage to move forward as well, without waiting for the laggard southern member states. Higher energy prices do not hamper successful and competitive economies; German energy prices are 41 per cent higher than those in Britain, Japanese 49 per cent, leading to higher investment in conservation and lower consumption in both countries.

Britain wastes energy; the domestic price of energy does not reflect environmental costs and resource depletion. We have some of the worst-insulated housing stock in Europe, while relative prices encourage industry to economize on labour more vigorously than on energy use. On the government's own figures, the Institute for Public Policy Research reports, British industry could reduce its consumption of energy by 20 per cent, without loss of output, by investing in energy-saving measures. Wasted energy in households, most of all in low-income households with poor insulation and inefficient heating systems, is estimated to range from 50 to 80 per cent of the total used.

The Conservatives have established an Energy Savings Trust to promote better insulation and economies in energy. Disputes with the gas industry and regulator over funding have, however, left it so far without the money to carry out its intended functions. Liberal Democrats would ensure adequate funding for energy conservation projects, from a levy (as the Conservatives had intended) on fossil fuel consumption; would provide grants and subsidies to industry to replace energy-inefficient plant and machinery; and would support further research and demonstration funding for renewable sources of energy. Liberal Democrat proposals to shift the balance between private and public transport will be outlined in Chapter Five.

Investment in environmental sustainability provides another virtuous circle of economic development. Most energy conservation work is labour intensive; estimates suggest that a £1 billion annual programme would directly create about 60,000 extra jobs. Support for industrial exploitation of environmental technology would give Britain comparative advantages in an expanding global market. The US Commerce Department reported in October 1996 that American exports of environmental technology had risen by 50 per cent in the previous year, with the active support of a federal inter-agency group and the Export–Import Bank; it would be tragic for Britain to allow this growing market to pass it by. Energy saving reduces imports and conserves domestic resources for the longer term. Investment in renewable energy sources has a high long-term return.

North Sea gas has given Britain plentiful supplies of cheap and relatively clean energy for the next ten or fifteen years, and made it also self-sufficient in energy supplies for the foreseeable future. Liberal Democrats want to use that window of opportunity to invest in improving energy efficiency and in renewable energy sources. Conservation and investment together could enable renewable sources to provide up to 20 per cent of electricity demand within fifteen years. We want in addition to phase out the remaining subsidies for Britain's nuclear industry, and will campaign for the removal of nuclear and fossil fuel subsidies throughout the EU. The British contribution to the reduction of carbon and other emissions on a global scale demands such an approach. But it would also be to Britain's economic advantage to follow this virtuous path.

FIVE

The Quality of Our Society

Good government, a soundly based economy and an open and inclusive society reinforce each other. Deterioration in one of these three elements damages the others. The fundamental purpose of democratic government is to provide the framework within which civil society can flourish. The market is not an end in itself, but the most effective mechanism yet discovered for maximizing individual choice, encouraging individual initiative and decentralizing property and wealth. Active government is needed to correct market distortions and prevent undue concentrations of power within market sectors. Active government is also needed to moderate the impact of economic and technological change on society, to ensure that the social order which contributes to a dynamic economy is not weakened or destroyed by the shock of transition.

Britain's society has radically changed since the Second World War. The welfare state was designed for families in which the husband worked and brought home the family income while the wife kept house, raised the children and often looked after the grandmother – sharing informal care with members of their extended family living close by: stable families, living within the same local community over a generation, with the male breadwinner in the same job for most of his working life. Discipline and respect were enforced on the younger generation by relatives and friends within close-knit communities. The postwar state as economic planner hoped to provide conditions of virtually full employment; its role as welfare provider was to tide such families over short-term unemployment, accident or tragedy. Few of the elderly lived much beyond seventy; pensions for retired workers and widows could thus be paid for through National Insurance without imposing enormous overheads on employment.

Seen through the rose-tinted spectacles of nostalgia, the 1950s are now depicted by Conservatives (and by some Labour spokesmen) as a golden age of social order, before the infection of liberal individualism swept through the land. Selective memory has blotted out the dependence of the old social order on the subjection of women: carers and home-makers, some trapped by economic dependence in unhappy marriages, many denied the chance to develop their own talents. Industrial transformation since then has swept away steady employment, above all for the skilled and semi-skilled workers who formed the traditional solid working class; new employment has often been 'women's work', in services and light industry. Affluence and economic change, the motor car and the suburban estate, have broken up local communities and dispersed families.

The greater mobility of labour which economic growth has brought, which admirers of the American model would like to quicken further, carries unavoidable social costs: no relatives round the corner to share childcare, fewer old friends to provide support when needed. Flexible labour markets imply looser social ties; governments which promote the first cannot simply stand back and deplore the second. Physical environment – houses and streets, shops and public spaces – also shape communities. Planners and architects, not civil libertarians, contributed most to the dissolution of social order in the 1960s, demolishing integrated communities and separating classes and generations into tower blocks and housing estates.

We could not put the clock back, even if we wished to. Liberal Democrats welcome the greater freedom which affluence has brought to so many, and the social revolution – still under way – which has given women wider choices and more control over their own lives. Better health, diet and housing have brought the benefit of longer life to most people. Cars, telephones, television and computers have altered social networks, weakening local ties while helping to maintain relationships among dispersed families. The social impact of economic and technological change has to be managed and moderated; it cannot be reversed.

Government alone cannot – and should not – set the terms for civil society. That way lies authoritarianism, enforced conformity, the exclusion of difference and dissent. But government action can strengthen or weaken the conditions for civil society, in many different ways. The physical structure and environment of communities is shaped by planning controls and government guidelines. These determine closeness to (or distance from) shops, to work and to public transport, set rules which favour bleak open spaces or courtyards and closes, densely packed terraces or widely spread houses, generous or limited provision of public spaces and public buildings. Work provides both income and status; communities with high levels of unemployment start to fall apart.

Solidarity between different groups is stronger where the gap between rich and poor is moderate, weaker when the gap is wide. People who lack work, security or participation in stable communities over long periods lack a stake in society. Policies of social inclusion therefore strengthen social order, and reduce crime. Tolerance of minorities and of social dissent promotes inclusive communities; government example and legal protection are both important. Not only bread, but also circuses, matter: the symbols of the state, the icons of national history and culture, the representation and reinterpretation of social memory and civilization through art, the role which education plays in transmitting social values and national identity from one generation to another, are all part of the essential contribution which government should make to the liberal aim of ordered civil society.

Building communities, maintaining communities

Britain is a crowded country: most of us live and work in towns and cities. Yet town and city centres have deteriorated in most of Britain over the past generation. The American phenomenon of middle-class flight from the cities to the suburbs, leaving cities to the poor and the unemployed, has been echoed in Britain in the construction of suburban estates and out-of-town shopping centres. Suburban sprawl across Britain's limited country-side, with multi-lane highways stretching across previously peaceful woods and farmland, carries, however, enormous costs to our environment. Public pressure has now at last forced transport engineers to think of limiting traffic to what the environment will bear, instead of building more roads to match the predicted increase in traffic. We must reclaim our cities as places in which to live well, to walk safely, to relax and enjoy ourselves, to find plentiful employment and to share a sense of civic pride.

Reclaiming our cities requires a long-term strategy, integrating a return to accountable elected city government with changes in planning policy, finance and local taxation, housing provision and transport. Nineteenth-century Britain built proud cities, with magnificent town halls, public parks, theatres and galleries. Centralization of power in London has transferred municipal services first into nationalized industries and then into privatized companies. Two-party politics operated to prefer social segregation, building massive single-class estates to form safe Labour or Conservative wards.

Planners also strove to segregate work from housing: removing people from city centres, creating new industrial estates and relying on massive flows of commuters to travel between these two separate worlds. The result has been wastelands of offices and shops, deserted and unsafe after dark, encircled by deprived and run-down council estates, with an outer ring of affluent suburbs. Patterns of property investment and property taxation have exacerbated this development – in contrast to the majority of continental cities, where mixed residential neighbourhoods have been maintained in the centre of cities.

Conservative policies have taken power and money away from Britain's cities. The Greater London Council and the other English metropolitan country councils were abolished in 1986. The first-past-the-post voting system had given Labour control of all of them, and Mrs Thatcher destroyed them rather than provide a more open electoral system which might have exposed them to shared political control. Michael Heseltine pointed out in 1984 that Conservative changes in tax and benefits had redirected £8 billion to the affluent regions of south-eastern England, while returning only £168 million to northern cities in regional support. The result has been an impoverishment both of cities as entities and of city-dwellers as individuals. A bewildering succession of 'urban initiatives' announced in London has made the problems worse, with 'challenge awards' forcing cities to compete against each other for limited funds against short deadlines. Integrated Regional Offices of central government, designated ministers for regions and cities, groups of appointed businessmen or Conservative supporters to substitute for democratic representation, consultants paid to discover what elected representatives could have told them, have all proved inadequate substitutes for self-government.

Liberal Democrats want to encourage more people to move back into city centres, to re-create mixed urban communities. The demand is there where suitable housing and facilities are provided, as the success of London's docklands and the conversion of warehouses in northern city centres show. Urban reclamation and refurbishment is a far better answer to demand for additional housing, as household sizes continue to shrink, than suburban sprawl across greenfield sites, creating extra commuting pressures and environmental damage, while leaving estate dwellers without cars imprisoned in their houses, far away from public transport and shops.

Urban regeneration will require coordination of a range of policy initiatives. That is best achieved through revived local self-government, within a broader regional framework – not by competing ministerial pronouncements from the centre. More of the tax revenue which cities generate should be theirs to spend, rather than being siphoned off to the Treasury to be packaged into ministerial 'initiatives'. City schools deserve special assistance. Local policing must be stepped up, to make city streets safe and give their inhabitants self-confidence. Public transport must be improved, and cars discouraged. The anonymity of the motor car and of its passing driver has contributed a lot to urban insecurity; recreating local neighbourhoods, where people walk between home, shops and workplaces, promotes familiarity, mutual recognition and so, in time, mutual trust.

Higher levels of urban employment are crucial; problems of crime and of school delinquency are concentrated in areas of high unemployment, most particularly in one-class council estates. Unemployment stirs racism, as competition for scarce jobs sharpens and unemployed youths form into gangs. The principles of planning in urban areas have to be reversed, to bring work, shops, entertainment and housing closer together and wherever possible to substitute socially integrated neighbourhoods for one-class housing estates. This is, inevitably, a long-term strategy; we cannot promise easy or immediate results. Britain's cities have been neglected for twenty years or more. It will take time to carry out the physical, economic and social repair work that is needed.

Shelter and security; better-quality housing

Conservative policies have had a radical impact on the country's stock of housing and its pattern of ownership. Much council housing has been sold off. Housing associations have mushroomed, partly replacing previous local authority functions in providing social housing. House prices rocketed during the 'Lawson boom' of the late 1980s, leaving many over-optimistic buyers with negative equity in homes for which they had borrowed more than the value they could recover.

Britain now has a higher proportion of its population in

owner-occupied housing than any other European country, and a lower proportion in rented housing. Homelessness has more than doubled since 1979. The private rented sector has shrunk further, leaving local authorities no choice but to accommodate families in bed and breakfast hotels, while unscrupulous landlords exploit both poor tenants and the social security Housing Benefit scheme.

Liberal Democrats would allow local councils to invest in new social housing by releasing their capital receipts from past council house sales, and by allowing them to raise finance on capital markets for investment. We would redirect tax privileges by phasing out Mortgage Interest Relief, and replacing it with a mortgage benefit scheme and a targeted Housing Benefit for those who have temporarily lost jobs and income. We would promote a larger private rented sector, through encouraging small-scale and institutional investment in rented housing; wherever possible we would involve tenants in managing their own areas and estates, and would reinforce moves towards community self-management through the establishment of 'urban parish councils' so as to provide a focus for sharing neighbourhood concerns and responsibilities.

Housing is closely interwoven with other areas of social policy. Housing policies cannot be seen in isolation; they overlap with employment policy, with preferred patterns of taxation and benefits, with land-use planning and with energy use. The Liberal Democrat approach, in this as in related policies in other areas, is to use the instruments available to central and local government to encourage people to look after themselves, and so to regain self-confidence and a shared sense of neighbourhood and local community.

Transporting people, tackling pollution

The development of road, rail and air transport within a crowded island cannot be left solely to market forces, responding to patterns of demand as they develop. The thrust of government transport policy, thankfully, has already sharply altered – under the pressures of repeated demonstrations by environmental protesters and the belated recognition that new roads and bypasses themselves generate additional traffic. The Department of Transport, which under Labour and Conservative governments alike continued to design and build roads to meet predicted patterns of traffic, while planning for long-term decline in public transport use and investment, has during the last two or three years accepted that the growth of private traffic must be curbed and public transport promoted. The process of privatizing buses and railways has, however, so far inhibited the definition of a new strategy.

A key function of transport planning must be to reduce traffic. Transport already accounts for a fifth of the UK's global warming emissions, and is now the only sector in which the output of emissions is rising. Transport planning of course relates closely to land-use planning; moves towards integrated neighbourhoods, a greater emphasis on urban housing, restrictions on the growth of out-of-town shopping centres, all contribute to a reduction in transport demand and to a shift towards journeys by bicycle and on foot rather than journeys by car. Urban streets should be pedestrian- and cyclist-friendly, not fast through-routes for cars. Liberal Democrats in local government have promoted pedestrianization and traffic calming measures; these not only reduce accidents, but also play a part in reducing crime.

Taxation has a role to play in altering incentives. The real costs of car travel have fallen over the past fifteen years, while costs of public transport have risen. Liberal Democrat proposals to speed up the fuel-tax accelerator (the commitment by the present government to increase fuel taxes cumulatively from year to year) would reverse the balance. We would press for agreement within the EU on higher aviation fuel tax, to reflect the environmental costs of aircraft noise and air pollution and to encourage transfer to rail. We support experiments in urban road pricing as a means of restraining traffic in city centres. Revenue from such charges should be used to support public transport.

Given that privatization of bus and rail companies is largely complete, we would use regulation and franchising – the provision of public money as subsidy in return for the provision of agreed services – as instruments of policy. The complexities of providing public subsidies to profit-making enterprises, which is how the Conservative Government has designed rail privatization, will make effective regulation vital. Franchises will have to extend over periods long enough to encourage companies to invest, with active regulation to ensure that public subsidies – from national government and in future also from regional and local authorities – support improvements rather than excessive profits and salaries. The strategic development of railway infrastructure should be a matter of national policy. Liberal Democrats therefore opposed the privatization of Railtrack, and will want to ensure that the next government reasserts effective control. Higher levels of investment in all forms of public transport – from urban tram systems to the West Coast Main Line – are needed. Wherever possible we will support partnership schemes between public and private finance; we would relax the outdated Treasury Rules which limit the ability of public sector trading companies to raise investment capital in the markets. The collapse of the government's road-building programme has led to a crisis in the construction industry and a sharp decline in public investment; we would apply the resources freed from these cutbacks to urban and national rail schemes.

Reclaiming our countryside

Britain's countryside has been subject to a range of adverse pressures over the past twenty to thirty years. Intensive farming has reduced agricultural employment and contributed to ground water pollution and soil erosion in many areas. Large-scale removal of hedgerows has altered the pattern of the land and impoverished wild plant and animal life. Rural services – buses, post offices, village schools and shops – have declined. Second-home owners and car commuters have weakened village communities; government-enforced sales of rural council houses have made it difficult for the less affluent to find housing when they have found work. Suburban housing, greenfield industrial sites and road- and motorway-building have eaten into Britain's stock of agricultural land; quarries and landfill sites have also degraded countryside areas.

The Liberal Democrat approach to rural revival aims to shift the emphasis of government support from agricultural production to stewardship of the land. We want a countryside policy, not just an agricultural policy. We recognize that the EU's Common Agricultural Policy (CAP) limits what British government can do on its own – but argue that the Ministry of Agriculture has interpreted the CAP inflexibly, to support the interests of large agricultural producers while cutting back on advice services for small farmers. It has paid far too little attention to issues of food safety, environmental sustainability and rural enterprise. The mishandling of the BSE crisis, from the end of the 1980s on, is only the most dramatic example of ill-considered policies badly managed.

Liberal Democrats would therefore dismantle the Ministry of Agriculture, in order to change the culture of government towards rural areas. Some of its functions should appropriately be transferred to the Departments of Health and Environment; others should be regrouped into a new Department of Natural Resources, which would itself take over some environmental and land-use planning functions from the Department of Environment. In place of the CAP we would move towards a common rural policy, in which agriculture would continue to play an important but not an exclusive role. A parallel reappraisal of CAP objectives and methods is already under way in other EU member states, and we see no difficulty in achieving this reorientation within the European framework.

Rural priorities should appropriately be determined as far as possible at regional and local levels, in partnership with central government. Existing programmes of support for environmentally sensitive areas would be expanded into a general system of

Countryside Management Contracts, negotiated with individual farmers, with public support conditional on conservation and sustainable agricultural methods, and with added incentives to move away from intensive farming towards 'extensification' and to expand organic methods. Our aim is to conserve a sustainably productive countryside, and to provide viable incomes for those who maintain it.

In country areas, as in cities, we favour redirection of planning rules to encourage integrated communities, in which work and employment are close to each other. That means encouraging the growth of small workshops in country communities, taking the opportunity to convert redundant buildings wherever possible. That also means encouraging local processing of countryside products, from milk to wood, and of 'distance working' through electronic communication. The revival of local government, to which Liberal Democrats are committed, will restore self-government – and a larger degree of self-financing – to Britain's rural areas; we will encourage local authorities to support community shops and to experiment with different forms of rural public transport. We will also support an active partnership between local government and the voluntary sector, which plays an essential role in rural communities.

City dwellers and country dwellers have different interests, which government must reconcile. Access to the countryside is an important principle for all, on private as well as publicly owned land; rights of access, and limits to access, should be openly negotiated within Countryside Management Contracts. Extensification of farming, and stricter controls on animal husbandry, will bring more animals back into the fields; higher standards of animal protection imply higher prices in urban shops. Enjoyment of wildlife can cut across necessary control of wildlife, if viable agriculture is to be maintained. Conservation has traditionally gone with shooting and fishing, and continues to form an important part of the rural economy. Tourism offers a valuable source of rural employment; local and central government should work together to encourage as wide a spread as possible. A balance has to be struck between sustainable methods of production, the conservation and re-establishment of habitats for wildlife and wild plants, and urban expectations of rural simplicity. Liberal Democrats favour a long-term doubling of the land area of Britain devoted to forestry – not only through the establishment of new forests but also through local woods contributing to local energy use and local industry.

Social order

'Neither crime nor policing can be considered in isolation,' the Police Superintendents' Association asserted in its submission to the Liberal Democrat working group on crime in 1995. 'They need to be considered alongside education, social deprivation, community development and drugs taking.' The breakdown in our communities partly explains the increase in lawlessness. So does the rise in long-term unemployment and poverty. The House of Commons Home Affairs Committee concluded in 1993 that 'there is obviously an unquestionable link in some cases between unemployment, hopelessness and crime'.

The battle against crime and the rebuilding of social order thus require both immediate measures and a long-term strategy. Liberal Democrats do not believe that the answer is to build more prisons, as Michael Howard was proposing in 1996. It has been estimated that higher mandatory sentences will mean an increase in the prison population from 57,000 (already the highest as a proportion of population in Europe) to 68,000, requiring a dozen new prisons and a sharp rise in the Home Office budget to pay for them. The only industrialized democracy which has a higher proportion of its population in prison than this is the USA, which also has by far the highest rate of crime.

Reported crime has doubled since 1979. The Conservatives' response to rising crime has been an unprecedented volume of criminal justice legislation – sixty Acts of Parliament in twenty years. Under Michael Howard its approach has become increasingly populist, responding to every newspaper campaign, and

attempting to put the blame on opposition parties for not supporting 'tougher' measures. At the same time money for crime prevention has been cut, and the probation service has been starved of
funds.

Liberal Democrats' immediate proposals for tackling this surge
of crime include:

- a much greater emphasis on crime prevention, through
  increased use of closed-circuit television, better lighting of
  public spaces and increased pedestrianization.

- local partnerships to improve security in crime-prone areas,
  through the recruitment of additional caretakers and super-
  visors and through closer links between the local community
  and the police.

- additional resources to enable police authorities to put an
  extra 3,000 officers on the beat, paid for in part from savings
  in projected funding for extra prisons.

- allowing police authorities to appoint a new category of
  'retained police officer', to extend and upgrade the role of the
  special constabulary.

- tighter controls on offensive weapons of all kinds.

- more effective national and international cooperation against
  organized crime, particularly the drugs trade; Liberal Democrats have strongly supported the establishment of Europol,
  against Conservative government objections.

- expanding and adequately funding the Victim Support Movement and the Witness Support Scheme, to rebuild confidence
  in the community that crime can be defeated.

The problems of crime cannot, however, be solved by law and
order policies alone. Fifty per cent of known offenders are under
twenty-one. A longer-term strategy to rebuild social order must
therefore include higher investment in education, including pre-
school education to give children from deprived and disordered
households an early start in learning how to cooperate with

others, and a reversal of the cuts in 'special needs' education for children with behavioural and other problems. It must also include targeted efforts to provide work experience for sixteen-to-nineteen-year-olds, in partnership with local employers. It should combine tougher action on truancy with closer cooperation between the police, the probation service, schools and social services.

Strong local communities, rooted in an inclusive national society and a thriving economy, are the only long-term defence against crime. Social order cannot be taught through a national formula imposed on poorly paid teachers in underfunded schools, coping with children from households in which no one is employed and few of whose neighbours are in work. Sink schools in sink estates breed delinquents; community schools in socially integrated communities breed citizens. Socially divisive policies over the past twenty years have undermined Britain's social order. Liberal Democrats will work to reintegrate British society, through every instrument of policy available to us at local and at national level.

A tolerant society, a diverse society

Britain has always been a diverse society. The English and Scots emerged out of long intermarriage between Celts and Saxons, Normans and Danes. We gave asylum to the Moravian and Huguenot Protestants in the seventeenth century, to Jews from Russia in the 1890s and from Germany in the 1930s. The first Africans and Indians arrived in British ports – and in the service of British aristocrats – in the late eighteenth century, the first Chinese a century later. The Second World War brought displaced Poles, Ukrainians, Lithuanians, Estonians; Commonwealth immigration in the postwar years brought much larger numbers from the Caribbean and the Indian subcontinent.

Britain has gained, economically and socially, from this repeated inflow of new energy and talent. It will serve us well in the global market in the next generation to have a society which accommodates different cultures. The pressure of world population growth, and of the sharp increase in international refugees and asylum seekers, has forced us to impose tighter restrictions on new entrants. But Liberal Democrats consider it vital that Britain makes the best of the diversity it has already achieved.

Liberal Democrats will strengthen legal redress against discrimination by incorporating the European Convention on Human Rights into domestic law. We will bring together the Equal Opportunities Commission and the Commission on Racial Equality, both combating discrimination which damages our society and economy, in a Commission on Human Rights, which would also have jurisdiction over discrimination against disabled people. We will reverse Conservative resistance to the extension of racial discrimination legislation to the European level, to ensure that the rights of black and Asian British citizens are fully respected throughout the EU.

We will also strengthen anti-discrimination legislation on behalf of gay men and lesbians. Sexual orientation, like religious belief, has historically been a cause for persecution; a tolerant civil society should accept and respect both. We will repeal Section 28 of the 1988 Local Government Act. We will create a common age of consent, regardless of gender or of sexual orientation.

Acceptance of the principle of equal rights and opportunities within a diverse society cannot be enforced by legal means alone. Leadership and working practices, in politics and in the public services, also count. A democratic voting system would bring many more women into Parliament and give much better representation of ethnic minorities, providing positive symbols for private employers and individuals.

The police have been slow to overcome traditional male prejudices, or to welcome ethnic minority recruits on equal terms; Liberal Democrat representatives on police authorities are using their influence to press for tougher action against examples of prejudice, and for in-service education. The armed forces have made remarkable strides in their acceptance of women in recent years. But Liberal Democrat influence in government would press for further progress in offering opportunities in the armed services to ethnic minorities, and would halt the actively hostile attitudes displayed to gay men and lesbians.

Disabled citizens should be enabled to participate as fully as possible in economy and society. Liberal Democrats will reintroduce the Civil Rights (Disabled Persons) Bills of 1994 and 1995, which were blocked by the Conservatives in the House of Commons. We will overhaul and simplify the complex system of disablement allowances and benefits, introducing a Partial Capacity Benefit to assist those able to undertake limited work. Many of the large number of carers in society who relieve pressure on the health and social services by looking after the sick and elderly suffer extreme financial difficulty. We would also replace the current Invalid Carer's Allowance with a Carer's Benefit, index-linked to average male earnings. This would not be counted as income in cases of Income Support and would be payable on top of earnings to those who spend a certain amount of time caring.

The Conservative government has played partisan politics over refugees, as over crime. Liberal Democrats insist that openness to genuine refugees has been a vital part of Britain's political tradition, and should remain so. We will work with our neighbours within the EU to agree a common European policy towards asylum seekers, sharing the costs of support equitably.

Health and long life

Liberal Democrats believe in the National Health Service and in its founding principle of a free service available to all and free at the point of need. Observation of other countries' provision persuades us that in spite of its current problems and constraints the NHS remains one of the most efficient and cost-effective providers of health care in the developed world. Our object is to improve it, not to destroy it.

We recognize that health involves wider issues than mere

standards of health. Poverty, unemployment, poor housing and environmental degradation all contribute to ill-health. Prevention is always better than cure; for that reason we support better health education, helping people to understand their own bodies, to prevent illness and to spot problems earlier. Linked to this we would foster healthy living, which helps avoid illness not just by promoting exercise and better nutrition, but by giving incentives to encourage people to change habits. One such approach is to build safe cycle lanes in towns and cities; this would both promote exercise and at the same time reduce the use of polluting motor vehicles. Conversely, government action can discourage unhealthy activities, for example by further increases in tobacco taxes and banning cigarette advertising.

However good our systems of prevention are, people will still need health care, and the NHS will remain the most efficient provider. There has been a profound change in the way health services are organized and health care is provided since 1992. We are critical of some of these changes, but we recognize that any further major upheaval in the health service would lead to lower morale and impede the NHS's ability to care for patients. Our principles are that, wherever possible, primary care should be given priority over secondary care, and that resources should as far as possible be shifted from administration back to direct services to patients.

Tory reform of the NHS has failed in several ways. It has not given patients more choice; it has not reduced costs; beds have been lost and hospitals been closed *before* other community-based services have replaced them. Along with many health care officials, we favour separating the roles of commissioning and providing health care. This system would be more open, flexible and cost-effective than existing practice, since those responsible for commissioning would push hospitals to provide the services needed by the community rather than those which consultants want to provide.

Liberal Democrats want to promote a closer working relationship between local health authorities and social services departments; we would eventually like to merge these as part of a fundamental review of local government. We would also create regional health and social services authorities, made up of representatives from the relevant authorities. This change would facilitate cooperation between primary-health-care providers – GPs and other community health services – and social services.

A third of GPs covering 40 per cent of patients are now fundholders. Fundholding GPs can secure the services they want for their patients, unconstrained by the rules of the internal market and are allocated funds in a different way from non-fundholders. This results in a two-tier health service and makes long-term planning by health boards more difficult. We therefore propose to extend fundholding to *all* GPs, with a unified system of funding. We support parallel experiments in larger primary-health-care centres, aiming to provide a fuller range of services to their patients.

Liberal Democrats believe that we should get value for money from the health service, but unlike either Labour or the Conservatives we are interested in efficiency *and* quality. Currently the internal market in the health service is based on price competition; we believe that quality should also be taken into consideration. Since assessment of quality is partly subjective, we want individual patients to have as much say as possible in the services they receive and how and where and when they are delivered.

Health-service providers such as NHS Trusts are over-administered, and not publicly accountable. Liberal Democrats would reduce administration by extending annual contracts – which of course require repeated negotiations – to three-year periods. We are alarmed by the projected shortage of nurses, and will take immediate steps with the nursing profession to improve recruitment and training, to raise the morale of those working in hospitals and to attract non-working nurses back to the service. We also intend to make NHS Trusts more directly accountable to the commissioning bodies, and to increase local representation on Trust boards.

Advances in technology and an ageing population mean that

health-care costs rise faster than the rate of inflation. Although Britain's spending on the health service rose from 3.9 per cent of GDP in 1960 to 6.2 per cent in 1990, our spending remains the lowest in the European Union. Liberal Democrats know that increased funding of the NHS is necessary, but we are also convinced that the utility of expenditure must be assessed. Moreover, we are aware that funding from general taxation alone will not be enough to cover the increasing demands of the health service. We therefore propose to introduce hypothecated, or earmarked, taxes which we would guarantee to spend on specific services. In particular, a tobacco tax would be levied to help pay for health services. Just five pence on every packet of cigarettes sold would raise £200 million, enough to pay for the abolition of eye and dental charges. A tobacco tax would have the additional benefit of discouraging smoking, which, although diminishing the yield of this tax, would have long-term beneficial effects on the health of the nation and so cut health-care costs.

Supporting senior citizens

Liberals under David Lloyd George introduced the first state pensions at the start of this century; Liberal Democrats still support the concept of state pensions and seek to reform them to suit the twenty-first century. Changing demographic patterns mean that the number of people of pensionable age will rise by 50 per cent in the first thirty years of the next century. Thus far-sighted policies are needed to take this pattern into account. We believe that there must be a basic state pension, which provides a minimum standard of living for *all* retired people. We would end the contributory nature of state pensions, which has meant that many people who have been very low paid or had irregular patterns of work suffer poverty during retirement.

Liberal Democrats favour integration of income tax and National Insurance payments, but with a tranche which is earmarked for pensions which will provide benefits for all permanent UK residents. We recognize that both the public and private sectors have a role to play in providing pensions: we feel that while the state should provide the basic pension, private schemes are better suited to providing an earnings-related element. A Liberal Democrat government would therefore transfer responsibility for earnings-related pensions from SERPs to the private sector.

Social values, social culture

Man does not live by bread alone. A civilized society values its past, its culture, its common memory. Education is not just a matter of school work; public monuments, museums, the institutions of national cultural life, all contribute to our sense of shared identity and of national community.

Conservative policy is moving towards dependence on the national lottery, as a form of voluntary taxation, to fund an increasing proportion of cultural activities and conservation. National committees distribute these funds according to national criteria, with disproportionate amounts going to London and the English south-east. Liberal Democrats believe that national and local governments share a duty to support cultural life and communal heritage. Restoration of local autonomy to local government would help to strengthen centres of excellence outside London, developing partnerships between local governments, regional authorities and regionally based companies.

The BBC has become one of Britain's most valuable centres of cultural excellence and transmitters of national culture in accessible form. It also provides a symbol of British culture to audiences abroad – and usefully contributes to British exports. Liberal Democrats will maintain government support for an autonomous BBC, as broadcasting moves through the technological revolutions of multiple satellite channels and digital broadcasting. We seek, here as elsewhere, to maintain a balance between open access to what the global market can offer and support for high-quality British inputs which pay particular attention to British needs.

Privatization, cost-cutting and national heritage cut across each other. Another of the many contradictions of Conservatism post-Thatcher is the coexistence of continuing destruction or selling off of national assets with the rhetoric of nationalism and defence of the constitution. Liberal Democrats regard the piecemeal selling off of the historic buildings of the crown estate in Whitehall, starting with the proposed conversion of the Treasury buildings into leased offices, luxury apartments and a hotel, as beyond reasonable justification. This is the core of British government, owned by the crown for hundreds of years. Strong government pressure on private companies to sponsor the Greenwich millennium exhibition came close to involuntary taxation, and confused national objectives with private interests. British governments are temporary stewards of the British state, its institutions, property and traditions – not directors of a company who attach little importance to its long-term survival. Liberal Democrats insist on the principle of stewardship, which Conservatives now appear to have forgotten.

SIX

The World We Live In

A rapidly changing world requires a redefined British foreign policy. Nostalgia for an imperial past, combined with hostility to closer cooperation with Britain's neighbours, offers no credible way forward. Our starting-point for a more constructive, forward-looking international approach is to build coalitions of like-minded governments, first within Europe and then beyond; and to work with them to strengthen international institutions and to negotiate and implement the common policies needed to promote sustainable economic development and a stable and secure global order.

Liberal Democrats are internationalists by instinct and by intellectual conviction. The tasks we now face in managing our shrinking world, in which economic and environmental developments are on a global scale, demand a cooperative response from states working together. The British contribution to global stability and prosperity, to combating threats to global order and to the global environment, is most effective when combined with the contributions of other democratic European countries. We believe that Britain can achieve more through sharing sovereignty and pooling power than through standing alone.

Britain is a European country. Our international interests and responsibilities start with our concern to promote peace, stability and prosperity within Europe, in partnership with our European neighbours. There's nothing startlingly new or radical about this statement, however unwilling Eurosceptics and right-wing newspapers are to admit it. Sixty per cent of Britain's overseas trade is with the other members of the European Union. We stationed four divisions of the British army, and a large part of the Royal Air Force, in West Germany throughout the cold war, as Britain's contribution to the common defence; one division and seven squadrons remain there still. British companies now treat the European Union as their home market; two of Britain's largest companies (Unilever and Shell) are jointly owned Dutch–British enterprises. With the Conservative government's blessing continental companies in recent years have bought into Britain, with Rover – the last British-owned car manufacturing company – now owned by BMW, with German and Dutch banks major players in the City of London and privatization bringing railway lines and water supply under French ownership. Britain's 'special relationship' with the United States depended upon British commitment to Europe for its importance, with successive US administrations pushing British governments towards closer cooperation with France and Germany.

Britain's four most important neighbours and allies are Germany, France, the USA and the Netherlands. These are also Britain's four largest trade partners. Behind the nationalist rhetoric, British foreign policy has operated within a European framework for twenty-five years. The British Foreign and Commonwealth Office now exchanges officials with its French, German and Dutch counterparts; we even share embassy facilities with the Germans in several countries. A close Franco-British defence dialogue has developed over the past four years, building upon the experience of their forces in the 1991 Gulf War and in Bosnia; British forces in Germany now serve with German, Dutch and other troops in the NATO Rapid Reaction Corps under integrated command. The contradiction between growing practical cooperation and hostile political rhetoric has, however, confused and antagonized our partners, and undermined Britain's influence and reputation – not only in Europe but also in Washington.

Why Vote Liberal Democrat?

Liberal Democrats would make the best of Britain's international position, not the worst. There is a crowded agenda for European cooperation, and much to do to make the European Union more effective, less interfering and more democratically accountable. There are urgent tasks for international cooperation outside Europe: in managing the world economy, in tackling the threat of global climate change, in coping with the surge of refugees, in helping weak states and channelling assistance to countries and regions which are stuck in a cycle of rising population, deteriorating environment and worsening poverty. None of these tasks could be pursued effectively by a government which stood apart in nationalist isolation.

British foreign policy since 1989 has been built upon disguising from the public how far the international environment has changed, while hoping that foreign governments will not object too strongly to the gap between domestic presentation and international action. The Franco-British defence dialogue was conducted in the strictest secrecy for its first eighteen months, because the British government was reluctant to justify this departure from Thatcherite orthodoxy to its own backbenchers. Cuts in the Foreign Office budget were imposed without cutting back on declared ambitions; ministers disguised from Parliament that embassies were being opened in former Soviet states in premises provided by the Germans to gain some representation at minimum cost, even approaching British companies to ask them to subsidize British representation and contribute to the cost of Britain hosting international conferences. The Foreign Office budget is now smaller than that of the Intelligence Services; the BBC World Service and the aid budget have been cut back more sharply than defence spending.

The government has been trying to keep up appearances, rather than asking what we need now for a foreign policy to fit Britain's priorities after the cold war. Foreign policy is a field in which the Liberal Democrat commitment to open government and effective parliamentary accountability would pay immediate dividends in closing the gap between the presentation of policy and the practice.

Building a wider Europe

By the time a new government takes office, the 1996–7 Inter-governmental Conference (IGC) will have completed most of its work and be moving towards a revision of the Community treaties. Sadly, the obstructive approach adopted by the Conservative government will have reduced British influence over the outcome, and missed out on opportunities to build alliances with like-minded governments to push the EU in a direction which best suits British interests. Nevertheless we believe that it will be in Britain's long-term national interests to accept and ratify what has been agreed. The whole history of Britain's relations with European institutions has been of missed opportunities; initial reluctance to take part in negotiations, refusal to join each new initiative as it is launched, only to come in later complaining that the rules which others have agreed don't quite fit British preferences. It is likely that the EU will move on to another IGC within the next five to six years, as the continuing transformation of Europe from the divided continent of the 1970s and 1980s reshapes the whole region. A strong Liberal Democrat presence in Parliament will ensure that Britain plays a much more active and positive role in preparations for further reform.

Liberal Democrats strongly supported Chancellor Kenneth Clarke's insistence, against the opposition of other members of the Conservative Cabinet and party, that Britain should remain engaged in negotiations over a single European currency. The British economy will be directly affected by a move to a single currency whether we stay out or join. Given the achievement of a single European market and the increasing integration of Western Europe's domestic economies, the principle of a single currency is sound. Again, *we* would have negotiated actively to promote terms and conditions for a single currency best suited for Britain and for European expansion. We remain concerned that the Germans have – under domestic pressure – insisted on attaching conditions to monetary union which may prove too restrictive, holding down economic recovery and hindering new employment.

It is clear that most of the other EU members intend to join EMU. It would be as great a mistake for Britain to stay outside as it was for an earlier Conservative government to stay out of the European Economic Community in 1957. (The Liberal Party was the only party which argued for British membership in 1956–7, on the same grounds of long-term interests and international commitment.)

The management of monetary union will not be fixed irrevocably on day one; it will evolve with experience, as those represented in the European Central Bank and in its dialogue with the Council of Economic and Finance Ministers develop initial principles into working practices. Far better for British representatives to be taking part in those discussions rather than complaining from outside, while the Euro displaces the pound as the currency in which British banks and companies transact their European business and the City of London reorients itself towards the new regional currency.

The decision whether or not to join monetary union is thus both an economic and a foreign policy choice. It may well have to be taken within weeks of a new government coming into office, and will set the tone of that government's foreign and economic policy as clearly as did the Wilson government's decision to maintain the fixed pound–dollar exchange rate on coming into office in 1964. Liberal Democrats have made clear to British voters why we think it is in Britain's interest to join, and we will use our influence over a new government to bring Britain in among the first group to launch monetary union. The economic arguments have already been discussed in Chapter Four. In foreign-policy terms, to stay out (while even Ireland and Portugal may join) is to accept that Britain will move more and more to the edge of European cooperation, like Switzerland, Norway and Iceland, having to accept the rules which others negotiate and preferring national autonomy to international influence. But Britain is not a small state with limited interests;

our economic and political interests across the board are best served by ensuring that Britain becomes one of the core countries negotiating the future direction of European integration and the reshaping of Europe's role in world politics.

Monetary union is not the only vital issue on the European agenda – as British press coverage has portrayed it throughout 1996. Enlargement of the EU, and of NATO, to bind the former socialist states between Germany and Russia into a stable democratic, economic and security framework, is a major objective for the next ten years. Closer cooperation in foreign policy will be essential to manage relations with other states to the EU's east and south. A whole network of cooperation among police, immigration and intelligence services has grown up over the past twenty-five years, largely beyond public scrutiny or accountability either at the national or the European level. Further reform of the EU's imperfect institutions and working practices is needed to equip existing members to cope with extension across Eastern Europe, and to narrow the gap which has opened up between European institutions and the ordinary citizen in Britain and in other states.

Britain has played a constructive role both in preparing the associated states of Eastern Europe for enlargement and in adapting the EU to their entry. But we have left it to German companies to lead Western investment east, and to German and French ministers to lead in establishing political relationships. At the practical level the Foreign Office's Know-how Fund has provided one of the most useful programmes of technical assistance, while British military teams have also played a valuable role in retraining their armed forces; but there has been no link from these to any wider strategy. Liberal Democrats see the incorporation of these countries into a wider European Union as the highest foreign policy priority which Britain shares with its neighbours for the next few years. It is the key to the future stability of the European continent. It also offers Western Europe a rapidly growing market with which to trade, potentially raising our rate of economic growth as we help to raise theirs. Britain will share in the benefits, if government and business together make the best of the opportunity.

This is not a remote area for a country with its eyes firmly fixed away from Europe towards the USA and Asia, as many on the Right now believe. Britain failed to protect the Czechs in 1938, only to find itself at war over Poland in 1939. The breakdown of relations with the Russians over the future of Poland in 1945–6 was one of the developments which sparked the cold war, leaving thousands of Poles in exile in Britain. Yugoslavia was one of the most popular holiday destinations for British tourists fifteen years ago; the depth of public commitment remains evident in the wealth of private assistance efforts and in the welcome which British schools and voluntary groups have given to Bosnian refugees. Eastern Europe is now Britain's security frontier, and its emerging market. Britain and its partners failed to act together, or act early enough, when economic disputes and political rivalries stirred up ethnic tensions sufficiently to tear Yugoslavia apart in 1991–2, and are still paying the price of that failure. We should now do our utmost to ensure that the rest of the region successfully makes the transition from authoritarian socialism to liberal democracy.

Any effective British foreign policy now has to start by combining our efforts with our European partners' to influence others. In a UN of 185 member states, in which Britain now ranks eighteenth in GDP per head and tenth in overall GDP, we can no longer rely on the status we achieved as one of the world's victorious great powers in 1945. So long as the cold war continued, our strategic value to the USA and our closeness as a loyal junior partner gave Britain additional standing in Washington. But Ronald Reagan was the last of the pre-Vietnam generation, whose attitudes had been shaped in the Second World War and took it for granted that Britain was America's closest partner.

In the post-cold-war world American attention has turned away from Europe to other priorities. Within Europe the US administration has long seen Germany as its most important economic and political ally. Western policies towards Russia and towards the Middle East are now defined by the USA, then by Germany and thirdly by France, except when cooperation among Western European governments succeeds in agreeing a common position and acting upon it. The Conservative government's obstructive style and domestic preoccupations have sadly left Britain with only minor influence over these crucial issues.

Constructive engagement with our partners, instead of romantic isolation: that is the only way forward for a foreign policy which places a higher priority on contributing to a more stable and peaceful world than on leaving the prejudices of the right-wing press undisturbed. Largely unreported to Parliament or to the press, British ministers and officials have long since laid the foundations for a common foreign policy through regular contacts, shared secure communications and close cooperation in third countries and in international organizations.

The growth of intergovernmental cooperation among police and intelligence services provides the most glaring example of the gap between the rhetoric of national sovereignty and the reality of confidential joint activities – deliberately hidden from the public at home. The case for police cooperation across national borders is now strong. Fifty thousand British citizens now work in Germany; 250,000 own second homes on the continent in France, Italy and Spain, and almost 100,000 have retired to live in Spain or Italy. Thousands of citizens from continental countries – and beyond – work in Britain, thousands more come here to study, and millions come over on holiday every summer. Criminals, drug smugglers, illegal migrants mingle with them in the crowds crossing the frontiers; fraudsters switch funds by computer from one country to another. Characteristically, Conservative ministers have been at once enthusiastic to build closer links between national police and Intelligence agencies in response, and at the same time determined to keep it informal and secret, beyond the scrutiny of national parliaments or the European Parliament, without appeal to the European Court. There are major issues of civil liberties here, about which Liberal

Democrats care strongly. We would therefore have pressed in the current IGC to bring this field within the framework of the EU, and will use our influence in the next Parliament to ensure that the British government reports openly on the activities it is engaged in and the commitments it accepts.

Reshaping the European Union

The European Union itself is in need of reform. It was designed for six states forty years ago, to handle a limited number of common policies, few of which touched on central domestic political issues. It is ill-adapted to fifteen member states, now working together across most areas of domestic politics; and would come close to collapse under the impact of five, ten or more new members. Liberal Democrats want to cut back on the scope of Brussels regulation, which sets out to harmonize rules across Western Europe even on some economic and social activities which in the USA are left by Washington to the separate states. We apply John Stuart Mill's principle of 'the greatest dissemination of power consistent with efficiency' both inside and outside the United Kingdom.

Rural policies, as argued in Chapter Five, are for example much better moulded to national and regional circumstances than shaped by Europe-wide agricultural regulation. We therefore strongly support the Commission's efforts to reform the Common Agricultural Policy to take greater account of the diversity of agriculture across Western Europe and to bring prices closer to market levels, while leaving to national governments policy and finance for rural development. Environmental policy requires a partnership between different levels of government, from the local to the European; so does economic policy, setting the framework within the EU but leaving the detail to national governments and below. The EU budget should be reoriented away from support for agriculture to assistance to economic transition in Eastern Europe and transfers to disadvantaged regions within the EU.

The EU's institutions creak from complexity and outdated practices. We would cut back on the number of Commissioners and tighten the administration of the Commission itself. We hope that the Inter-governmental Conference will agree to a 'double majority' voting system for decisions among governments in the Council of Ministers. This would reflect the size of the populations which governments represent as well as the number of states voting. We do not share Conservative horror at extending the role of the European Court of Justice and the European Parliament; democratic accountability and the rule of law are not principles which should stop at national boundaries in a highly integrated Europe. We want to see more open policy-making, more public accountability and the acceptance and enforcement of clear rules for government, all the way from local authorities to the EU. Closer cooperation between national parliaments and the European Parliament provides one useful way to improve public visibility and accountability and to narrow the gap between Brussels policy-making and public understanding.

Sharing security, working for peace

Britain is now in the happy position of being freer from direct military threat than at almost any previous point in its history. Potential threats would strike Britain through our European neighbours; the most effective way to guard against them is therefore to work closely with our European neighbours. That is also the most cost-effective way of ensuring Britain's future security. European policy – strengthening and enlarging the EU, reshaping the North Atlantic Treaty Organization and the Organization for Security and Cooperation in Europe (OSCE) – *is* now the heart of British security policy. The future role of Britain's armed forcés has to be seen first in that context, secondly in the context of the appropriate British contribution to global peacekeeping and peace making.

The Atlantic Alliance – NATO – has been the core of Britain's defence policy since 1949. But NATO was designed to defend

Western Europe from the Soviet threat; it has therefore adapted its organization and functions since 1989, and will change further over the next ten years. The US Congress has become increasingly resistant to American spending on military commitments to Europe; European states are therefore having to take greater responsibility for their own security. Successive NATO meetings over the past four years have shifted the balance towards an alliance in which European states in 'combined joint task forces' will be expected to operate on their own in crises with American strategic and logistic support. British participation in the Rapid Reaction Force in Germany, and the transformation of the military relationship with France through shared experiences in the Gulf and Bosnia and through the Franco-British defence dialogue, have already taken our defence commitments much further towards the European framework for which Liberal Democrats argue than Conservative ministers would admit.

Bosnia has been the forcing ground for post-cold-war defence integration. This has been the biggest commitment of British forces abroad since the Gulf conflict of 1991, working within a multinational framework. Liberal Democrats argued for joint European intervention in Bosnia from the outset, when the British government was resisting French proposals to send a peace-keeping force. Had we and our partners gone in earlier and in sufficiently large numbers, we might have prevented some of the worst ethnic cleansing and the bitterness which it has left behind. Now that we are there we should stay, with our partners, until reconstruction is well under way and a degree of mutual trust has been restored.

The Bosnian experience also carries lessons for the future of British defence forces and defence policy. We need professional forces, sharing equipment as far as possible with our neighbours; France's recent defence reorganization has explicitly taken the British force structure as its model. The army has been stretched to maintain 10,000 troops and equipment in Bosnia at the same time as fulfilling its other obligations in Northern Ireland and Germany. It would be hard for any new government to find any further cuts in an already declining defence budget in the short term without damaging our capacity to contribute to and maintain such shared commitments.

In the longer term, however, it is as difficult to justify why Britain should spend twice as much on defence as Italy – which is much closer to most conceivable threats to the European region than Britain – as it is to justify continued American subsidies to European defence; both stem from past great power status more than present needs. There is no longer a British empire to defend, and there is a shrinking number even of colonial territories outside Europe to protect. Hong Kong is about to revert to Chinese sovereignty; the long-term security of the Falklands must rest on regional cooperation and improving relations with Argentina rather than on Britain alone. Northern Ireland, we must hope, will require fewer British troops in future years. The cost-effective way forward, maintaining credible forces while holding down spending, must be through closer integration of tasks, facilities and equipment with our neighbours. That is the direction in which British defence is, in effect, already moving, held back primarily by the nationalist rhetoric of Conservative ministers. Liberal Democrats, on the contrary, welcome this internationalist trend.

An international approach to British defence means strengthening European security integration within the Atlantic Alliance – far simpler now that France has rejoined the integrated NATO military structure – and linking that in turn to the development of a broader European common foreign and security policy. It means reinforcing bilateral military cooperation with the Netherlands, Germany, France and others, as well as reshaping and simplifying NATO's command structure to match integrated multilateral European forces. It means buying common equipment, and sharing training bases. And it means bringing defence more explicitly within the framework of common European foreign policy.

We recognize the need to cooperate as closely as possible with the USA; but we recognize also that European interests do not always coincide with American, and that British interests on most international issues are much closer to those of our European neighbours than to the USA's. American pressure to enlarge NATO eastwards has reflected Polish-American pressure and Washington officials' determination to maintain US leadership in the European region. Britain and its European partners have to be more concerned with how EU enlargement and NATO enlargement fit together, and how the two together contribute to overall European stability – including future relations with Russia, Turkey and the Middle East. Our priorities in relations with the Arab world and North Africa necessarily differ from those of the USA. What is to Washington a question of global strategy intermingled with the domestic politics of America's Jewish community is for Western Europe a relationship with a region which begins 15 km south of Gibraltar, against the background of Western Europe's ten million Muslims (a million of whom are British).

Britain has now invested in a new generation strategic nuclear system. In the absence of any clear and present danger, this should be maintained in a low state of readiness. Nuclear cooperation is already under discussion within the Franco-British defence dialogue; there is room to reduce costs through sharing patrols. There is no case for Britain maintaining an 'independent' nuclear deterrent as a badge of national status; the future of our nuclear forces, as of our conventional forces, should be determined in the context of multilateral negotiation over Europe's most appropriate contribution to global stability and order.

One of the greatest contradictions in Conservative policy over the past seventeen years has been the active support it has given to Britain's arms industry and to its exports overseas, while cutting back on support for civilian industry. This mistaken industrial policy – based upon close relations between the Conservative Party and the companies concerned, as well as upon the extraordinary Conservative assumption that Britain needed its own military industries to maintain its international standing, but need care little about the future of British-owned civilian industries – has left the British economy unbalanced. The determined sales drive has involved Britain in a succession of dubious relationships with authoritarian regimes, most scandalously with Iraq, but also including the misuse of overseas aid (for the Pergau dam) to support a package deal for arms contracts with Malaysia, and disregard for the occupation of East Timor in selling aircraft to Indonesia.

Demand for sophisticated weapons systems has fallen with the decline in international oil prices; supply has risen with surplus equipment and production capacity in the former socialist states. Alongside retrenchment and redeployment of British military production it makes sense to move towards tighter EU-wide restrictions on transfers of military and dual-use technology to non-democratic states, and to press for the transformation of the UN Register on Conventional Arms into a mandatory convention, with an effective verification process. The next British government must work with other governments to limit the global arms trade, not compete with others to sell arms in a shrinking market. Full British participation in the European Armaments Agency is in both our economic and our political interests.

Too many weapons are in international circulation; multilateral measures to control the arms trade and to promote disarmament must therefore complement national restructuring away from arms manufacture. Nuclear proliferation still threatens world stability; we support further negotiations to tighten controls on the diffusion of technology and the further reduction in the size of current nuclear arsenals. This is not, however, just a matter of major weapons systems. Liberal Democrats press for an immediate ban on the production of anti-personnel land-mines as well as their export and stockpiling, and for a similar Europewide ban; we must then work with our European partners to negotiate a global ban on their production or sale. Surpluses of small arms on international markets, left over from cold war arsenals, bring guns more easily within the reach of criminals and would-be terrorists. We will work to strengthen European controls on the production, storage and sale of guns, and to bring pressure on the USA and other states to tighten their domestic controls.

Working together to strengthen global cooperation

As in Europe, so across the globe – Britain's interests are best served by promoting cooperation and strengthening institutions. Global institutions are in urgent need of reform to provide the framework needed to manage our shrinking world. We recognize that Britain on its own has limited influence over global diplomacy. But Britain's voice in regional and global institutions still carries weight, when its arguments are well-founded and its influence concerted with like-minded partners.

The UN itself is in crisis. Over the past twenty years the United States has gradually shifted from being the UN's strongest supporter and financial contributor to become one of its most vigorous critics and its largest debtor. We recognize the urgency of reform of the UN and its agencies, and recognize also that the lead in reform must now be taken by European and Asian states – now the major financial contributors – in partnership. Britain's historical position as a permanent member of the Security Council gives us for the foreseeable future a privileged position in this reform process. We should use it to strengthen the European voice in global organizations, and to work through those global organizations to move their policies towards greater commitment to a sustainable world economy and a reversal of the widening gap between rich countries and weak, poverty-stricken states.

This is a matter of enlightened self-interest as much as of idealism. The world's fifty poorest countries now account for 2 per cent of global income (conventionally measured) while containing 20 per cent of its population. The global explosion in refugees, whose number has risen (on UN High Commission for Refugees figures) from 2.4 million in 1975 to 10.5 million in

1985 and 27.4 million in 1995, reflects the collapse or disintegration of states under the pressures of rapid population growth, deepening poverty, corrupt and incompetent government and international debt. It laps over into Europe, and into Britain, in the desperate struggles of refugees to escape persecution and starvation and build a better life for themselves through reaching the safety of the liberal democratic countries. Bad government, exploitation of natural resources for short-term gain, overpopulation, civil war and forced migration all imply environmental damage; we need competent governments with which to cooperate in moving towards shared global economic and environmental management. Corrupt government and desperate poverty fuel the global drugs trade, bringing organized crime into our cities. Epidemic diseases in overcrowded third-world cities can spill over into the rich world.

We will press together with our European partners to expand the agenda of the World Trade Organization (WTO) to include broader issues of global economic sustainability – as well as of human rights and the exploitation of labour. The *ad hoc* Committee on Trade and Environment should be made permanent. The so-far-inactive WTO Committee on Trade and Development should be pushed into action; an expert intergovernmental panel on trade and environment should also be set up, building on the model of the successful Intergovernmental Panel on Climate Change. The current WTO exemption clause allowing discrimination against goods made by prison labour should be widened to include forced labour of all types.

Beyond this, institutional reform of the proliferation of UN agencies is needed, to improve the coordination of related programmes, to economize on administrative overheads and to redirect priorities towards sustainable development and social change. The international financial institutions – the International Monetary Fund, the World Bank – follow far too strictly the doctrines of American economic orthodoxy. The structural programmes which the IMF imposes on debtor states press down harder on their poor through welfare cuts than on those who have benefited from accumulating foreign debt; concern for the quality of government and domestic society and for domestic environmental policies should also shape the conditions attached. Multilateral debt relief for the world's poorest countries – concentrated mainly in sub-Saharan Africa – is an essential part of enabling them to survive and recover. It makes little sense to extend repayment periods for debt incurred many years ago for countries whose economies are at the lowest level of development. Enlightened self-interest suggests that European states should take the lead in proposing that such debts should be cancelled and that further assistance should take the form of grants rather than loans. Social and political collapse in Africa brings refugees struggling to cross the Mediterranean, as European states have discovered over the past ten years; it is an investment in our own stability to help economic and political development in these weak states. Economic collapse is often also environmental collapse – as in Ethiopia and parts of West Africa – with long-term implications for our own environment.

Most policy towards developing countries must be made through multilateral channels, once we have a government committed to making multilateral cooperation work and to using shared European policies as the basis for wider global cooperation. But there are also particular contributions which Britain can make. Britain's multilateral and bilateral aid programmes are part of Britain's contribution to global security; but under Conservative governments they have shrunk from 0.5 per cent of GNP to 0.29 per cent, almost the lowest of any European country. Liberal Democrats would reverse those cuts, bringing British aid spending over ten years up to the UN-agreed target of 0.7 per cent of GNP. We would end the misuse of Britain's bilateral aid programme to support arms and construction contracts, and would untie it from purchases of British goods.

Extra resources would be channelled, through partnership with voluntary organizations, to local initiatives wherever possible. We would place particular emphasis on programmes which help to educate and emancipate women in developing countries, as leading to lower rates of population growth and supporting balanced social and economic development. We support and would implement the Overseas Development Administration's recommendation that 85 per cent of British aid should be concentrated on the twenty poorest states. In the emerging democracies of the former socialist world and in other less poverty-stricken developing states we should use limited funds to pass on the particular skills we have to offer in education, training and technical assistance – as the UK Know-how Fund is already successfully demonstrating in Eastern Europe. British initiatives where we have particular skills to offer, cooperation with others where that provides the most effective way to achieve our objectives: that is the Liberal Democrat approach to development policy, as to foreign policy as a whole.

SEVEN

The Choice This Time

This book has not attempted to persuade you that there are any easy answers to the problems with which Britain's political leaders will have to grapple over the next five years – let alone the next fifty. Nor has it pretended that the Liberal Democrats know all the answers; no one does. My aim has been to persuade you that the Liberal Democrats are, however, addressing the right questions, and that we open the door to a political dialogue which will bring disillusioned voters back into politics while shifting public attention to a new political agenda. We offer you the way towards a democratic renewal: a revival of local democracy, a Parliament freed from government domination, a looser party system, a freer flow of information.

Democratic renewal in turn opens the door to economic and social renewal – to a shift of priorities towards sustainable economic policies and towards reintegrating our fractured national community. Instead of the semi-presidential political competition of Blair versus Major, in which image and presentation obscure the artificiality of the campaign, an opportunity for wider choice and broader debate; instead of the politics of sound-bite and partisan attack, a more informed discussion of the issues at stake. That is the way to bring values and commitment back into politics, from the ground up rather than from the top down. That is the way to bring our disillusioned younger generation back to participate in democratic politics, as voters and party members. It requires a different style of political leadership, as well as a different style of politics: the willingness to listen as well as to guide, the commitment to explain as well as to set out choices, the courage to spell out the costs as well as the benefits of proposals and policies.

Your choice in this election will directly affect Britain's government over the next five years. But – as this book has argued from its opening pages – five years is far too short a period to shape or reshape our public institutions, our patterns of public spending, our economy or society. You need political leaders who are willing to look much further ahead, to anticipate future problems and to take steps to prepare for them. And you deserve political leaders who will not pretend that deep-seated social and economic weaknesses can be repaired by a few short-term measures. It will take far more than five years to build up our educational system to be as good at all levels as those of our foreign competitors. It will take more than five years to repair the damage to our communities, our cities and our social fabric which has contributed to the rise in crime. It will require long-term investment in buildings, equipment and – above all – people to ensure that our health services can meet predicted rises in demand. It is wise to shift the balance of our tax system away from employment to exploitation of energy and natural resources over an extended period, allowing citizens and companies time to adjust. So the intelligent voter will look beyond the personal appeal of each party leader and the immediate promises of the different manifestos, to consider how far each leader and party will attempt to shift public attention and policy-making structures to invest for future needs.

Conventional politics appeals to individual interests: offering you the promise of tax cuts, rising incomes and house prices, personal benefits from public policy. The politics Britain needs should revolve around national interests: public benefits as well as private, serving enlightened self-interest rather than immediate advantage. The health service you may need yourself in twenty-five or thirty years' time will only be there to help you if it is maintained – in the immediate interests of others – in the interim.

Why Vote Liberal Democrat?

You cannot assume that the economy will be strong enough to pay you a comfortable pension unless investment in education equips each new generation to compete in a changing world market. You cannot look forward to peaceful walks in familiar countryside, or friendly encounters in city centres, unless far-sighted government acts to protect them.

Elections provide national choices; but they take place within a European and global context. British security, British prosperity, the future of our island's climate and the level of the sea around its coasts all depend upon the cooperation of other governments. Nationalist reassertion may offer immediate though illusory self-satisfaction. Enlightened self-interest suggests that it is more useful to invest in winning the trust of Britain's neighbours and in strengthening international institutions. It's dangerously easy to appeal to popular mistrust of foreigners; but it's vital for political leaders and active citizens alike to argue against such populist appeals. Britain is a small and densely populated country – 55 million people in a world of 5.5 billion. Good government here requires active concern for good government in other countries and continents, taking our share of responsibility for global stability and global order.

Political choices, once you go into them, can't be reduced to six-word slogans or five-point programmes. It's a necessary part of mass campaigning that parties and political leaders are forced to simplify, to compress complex issues into deceptively simple formulae to attract the attention of a half-interested electorate. This book has examined some of the complexities which lie behind the competing slogans and programmes of the 1997 election, and set out the Liberal Democrat approach to the issues at stake. If you are persuaded that we have the right approach, do come and help us persuade others within Britain's confused and mistrustful electorate. With your help, and that of a great many others, we can and we will transform British politics.